THE FIRST THINGS OF JESUS

THE FIRST THINGS OF JESUS

OF JESUS

BY

JOHN REID

KREGEL PUBLICATIONS
Grand Rapids, Michigan 49501

Library of Congress Catalog Card Number 72-112362
ISBN 0-8254-3605-2

First American Edition published by
Kregel Publications, a Division of Kregel, Inc., 1970.
Reprinted from James Clarke and Co. Ltd. edition,
London. No date.

PREFACE

In the Gospels there are certain sayings of our Lord which are marked out as of special importance by the term " first." They tell us some of the things which He set above all others. They are illustrations of the moral perspective of Jesus, and it is this fact which gives unity to the separate studies contained in this book. But the student soon discovers that it is not in these instances alone that His precepts differ from the common thoughts of men. Everywhere His thoughts are higher than our thoughts. " Never man spake like this Man."

The studies are arranged in the following order :—(i) Sayings which refer to Jesus or His work ; (ii) Sayings which refer to His claim of authority and the supremacy of the Gospel ; and (iii) Sayings which contain precepts bearing on life and conduct.

In the revision of the proofs, the author gratefully acknowledges the assistance he has received from the Rev. Thomas S. Dickson, M.A., Edinburgh.

CONTENTS

First Bind the Strong Man

"I have spent forty years in making futile resolutions."—DR. SAMUEL JOHNSON.

"What men want is not talent, but purpose."
BULWER LYTTON.

"William the Silent, founder of the Dutch Republic, whose iron endurance overcame the power of Spain, is reported to have said, 'Before I entered upon this work I made a close alliance with the King of kings.'"

"Do you know the Persian legend, how the lover knocked at the door of his beloved, and the beloved said, 'Who is that?' He replied, 'It is I.' And the one inside said, 'There is not room for two.' Then he went away and came back after a year and knocked again. Again from the inside the voice said, 'Who is that?' But this time he answered, 'It is thou.' So the door opened and he went in."—E. F. BENSON, *The Challoners*.

THE FIRST THINGS OF JESUS

CHAPTER I

"FIRST BIND THE STRONG MAN"

THE appearance of Jesus as a teacher, in a sphere which the Scribes and Pharisees regarded as peculiarly their own, attracted their attention from the beginning of His ministry. He had passed through none of their schools, and was recognised by none of their authorities. Their watchful interest quickly turned into suspicion, and suspicion rapidly ripened into hostility. His growing popularity seemed to threaten their own influence and the ideals of national hope and religion which they passionately cherished. For the sake of the sacred interests which were in their charge, they came to the conclusion that His power over the people must be destroyed. His popularity was thought to be the result of His wonderful cures. It was these which had laid a spell upon the ignorant. The deepest impression had been made by the restoration to health of men and women who were thought to be " possessed with demons." Whatever was the actual character of this disease, it was at that time attributed to Satanic agency. This belief gave the Pharisees the opportunity of suggesting that His cures had been wrought by the same power. They said, " He casteth out demons by Beelzebub, the Prince of the demons " (Matt. xii. 24). It was a diabolically clever accusation. To an ignorant and superstitious people it would seem most credible. To get power over them, Satan might appear as " an angel of light."

The Pharisees had resorted to a similar slander once before. They had cast it at John the Baptist (Matt. xi. 18), with what effect we know not. Jesus, however, would not let it pass. For the sake of the simple folk who might be disturbed by such a charge, He set Himself to answer it. What did this accusation mean, that He cast out demons by Beelzebub ? It meant that Satan was casting out Satan ! It was as if a house or a city or a kingdom were divided against itself—one division fighting against another. That was the certain way to ruin and desolation. The Devil, with all his faults, was not a fool ! He would not build up his power with one hand and pull it down with the other. As a matter of argument, the answer was complete.

But Jesus goes on to suggest another explanation of His wonderful works. He said, " How can one enter a strong man's house, and spoil his goods,

First Bind the Strong Man

except he first bind the strong man ? " (Matt. xii.
29). The demoniacs were the " goods " of Satan,
the strong one. They could only be set at liberty
when a stronger than he had overcome him. The
cures which Jesus had wrought were the evidences
of His victory. Therefore, the kingdom of God
had come, the reign of the Prince of Darkness was
over. They who criticised and opposed the Victor
were guilty of unbelief and rebellion. Thus, the
charge against Him became an accusation against
them.

But the words of Jesus are more than a defence.
As in other instances, this answer of His becomes
a revelation of His mind and method. It tells us
something of the secret of the Messiah. We need
not discuss the relation of Jesus to the common
beliefs of His time regarding Satan and the kingdom
of darkness, or ask if He simply personified the power
of evil, or regarded it as embodied in a mighty
personality. The spiritual significance of His words
is plain. They are the symbolical enunciation of
a great truth which received its supreme illustration
in the life of Jesus, and is of the highest importance
as a guiding principle for all who follow Him. Before
one can enter a strong man's house and spoil his
goods, he must first " bind " the strong man ; that is,
before we can deal effectively with results, we must
deal with their causes. Evil must be conquered

in its seat of strength, before any real redemption from its power is possible or complete. The master of the slaves of sin must be overthrown before his rule can be broken. Jesus says, "This is what I have done." His cures were the proofs and trophies of a victory which had been already secured. They were the spoil of the strong man's house.

1. We believe that our Lord was referring to the Temptation as the occasion when this great victory was won. It was the first experience through which He passed after the Baptism. Its place in the story of His life is not an accident. It was the "knightly vigil" of the Messiah. It was the necessary trial to which He must submit before He could enter upon His work of redemption. Certainly if the words spoken here are connected with the Temptation, that experience receives a much deeper significance than is usually given to it. On the surface it was a trial as to the methods of the Messianic ministry. Each onset of the Tempter was an effort to induce Jesus to say or do something which was inconsistent with His mission, or with the spirit in which it was to be carried on. But a deeper question was involved than that of methods. The Temptation was in reality a conflict in the mind of Jesus as to who was to be the ruler of His life. Was He to trust God only, or was He

First Bind the Strong Man

to serve two masters ? Were suggestions of evil, even in their most necessary and plausible forms, to affect His actions ? Was His eye to be single, and His whole body full of light, or was His vision to be darkened by any admixture of evil ? The question involved the unity of His allegiance, and the purity and power of His life. Jesus saw the gulf which separated the way of faith from the way of unbelief ; the service of God from the service of Satan. To yield to evil in the slightest degree was to own to a double rule. It would mean that the will of the Messiah was divided ; that He was to use Satan to cast out Satan, and evil to oppose evil. He would have to say

> "I have submitted to a new control
> A power is gone which nothing can restore." *

The struggle was prolonged and intense, because the temptations came in a seemly and reasonable shape. In form they are not such as are common to men. They were the temptations of the Messiah, but they had in them all the might and glamour of all the trials of the soul. Jesus was suffering from the pangs of hunger, and was conscious of power to make the stones of the Wilderness bread. The power was given for the purposes of the Messiah —might He not use it for personal necessities ? What could He do for the Kingdom if He died of

* Wordsworth.

hunger ? The Jewish people expected that the Kingdom would come with power and great glory —ought He not to accommodate Himself to their hopes, and win a ready allegiance, by appearing as the Son of Man from heaven ? By such an act the Kingdom might come in a day. The kingdoms of the world were established by force and fraud and skill—was it possible to establish the Kingdom of God in any other way ? To " do a great good " might He not " do a little wrong ? " Could He not use the methods of the world to overcome the world, employing them for unworldly ends, and triumph over Satan by the powers in which he trusted ?

These were the questions around which the conflict raged, but when it was over the result was decisive. Jesus saw that beneath the question of method, there lay the deeper question of allegiance. He opposed each temptation, not with the presentation of another method, but with the declaration of His loyalty to God. He repelled every onset with the affirmation of His faith. He held to His trust in God throughout. Absolute dependence on His power, and absolute obedience to His will —these were His choice, His methods, and His might. Compromise was fatal ; self-will was weakness ; distrust was sin. They involved subjection to the power of evil, entanglement in its snares,

First Bind the Strong Man

and certain failure to realise His mission. Satan could not cast out Satan. Evil could not be used in the advancement of good ; the world's ways could not overcome the world. Jesus emerged triumphant from the critical conflict. Inward harmony was preserved by the complete rejection of everything that was alien to the will of God. He had definitely and finally chosen His side. He had determined from the outset who was to be the one ruler of His life. Milton, it may be, was nearer the truth than is commonly supposed, when he made the Temptation the subject of *Paradise Regained*. The poet may be a better guide to the essential facts and experiences of the life of the Messiah than the theologian. The victory in the Wilderness was critical and decisive. Failure there would have meant failure all along the line. Success contained within it the assurance and promise of the victory of the Garden and of the Cross. Jesus had " bound the strong man." Freedom from evil was to be the secret of His strength ; an undivided allegiance the source of His wisdom ; unworldliness the might of His influence on the world.

We faintly express the significance of these great truths when we repeat the lines

> " My strength is as the strength of ten
> Because my heart is pure."*

* Tennyson.

The First Things of Jesus

The sinlessness of Jesus is a fact of such uniqueness, that it is impossible for us to estimate its influence, or to measure the outgoings of its might. It is the source of His authority in all the aspects of His work. " Mightiest among the holy, and *Holiest* among the mighty, He has lifted empires from off their hinges with His pierced hands, and turned the streams of history into new channels, and still governs the ages."*

We recognise that there is a profound connection between sin and disease, although we may not always be able to trace it. Is it unreasonable to suppose that there is an equally profound and untraceable connection between freedom from sin, and the power to heal disease ? That is a fascinating and suggestive question, and an answer in the affirmative may lie at the basis of any satisfactory explanation of the cures which Jesus wrought. They are the " works " of one whose nature was untrammelled and undefiled by sin ; whose knowledge was undimmed, and whose powers were unweakened by a divided allegiance.

However it may be with regard to His miracles of healing, we certainly know that it is the sinless character of Jesus which has created the deepest sense and loathing of sin in the hearts of men, and made redemption from it a passionate desire. His

* J. P. Richter.

purity is the measure of His power ; His separation from sin has lifted Him to a position from which He draws the world unto Himself. It was as conqueror of evil that He became the Saviour of men. His victory was a great event in the spiritual world. Not for Himself alone was the conflict borne, or the victory won. From the day on which He returned in the power of the Spirit from the Wilderness, hope has shone for the hopeless, and a gospel of salvation has become the treasure of the world. The most degraded of the slaves of sin can find liberty in Him. The " strong man " has been " bound "; the doors of his prison-house are open, and *whosoever will* may come forth to the freedom wherewith Christ makes free. But the slave of sin must be ready to become the " free man " of Christ. In the spiritual world there is no compulsory liberation. The persons of men may be emancipated by Act of Parliament, but the liberty of the soul has to be chosen and claimed. Jesus will drag no unwilling captive from the horrible pit and the miry clay. Every motive and impulse that can quicken the desire for liberty is supplied, but the sinner must come to a definite and personal decision before deliverance can be accomplished.

2. The secret of a true Christian life, lies in an experience in the soul of the believer, somewhat similar to that of Jesus in the Temptation. There

are critical moments in the lives of men, when the future is determined. Two voices speak in the heart ; two ways are open to the choice, and two rulers claim allegiance. A decision is made between them, though there may be little consciousness of it. It may be a victory or a defeat which merely strengthens good or evil in us ; or it may be the decisive turning-point in life. It is by such a decision that conversion is accomplished. The question of the soul's allegiance is definitely settled —a full surrender of the will is made to Christ. Sometimes the crisis comes early, and is passed through without the sense of strain ; sometimes it comes late and is an agony. But the strength and peace of the Christian life depend on the thoroughness of the initial decision of the soul. The lack of this is an abiding cause of weakness, backsliding, and failure. The beginning has not been made in the right way ; one master of the soul has not been chosen : the " strong man " has not been "bound." The movement to Christ may have arisen under the impulse of an emotion which gradually fades, or a sin may be forsaken because it is seen to be hostile to the true interests of life. But the permanent changes of life are not the results of impulse or reason. They are the outcome of definite decisions of the will. There is a place for feeling and thought in the movement of conversion, but they are not the regal or the binding influences. It is the will that rules, and it is by it that Christ is chosen as the only ruler of the life.

Conversion, however, is not to be thought of as the act of man alone. The very word itself teaches us better. It is not " version," a turning, but " conversion," a turning with another. The emphasis must be laid on the first syllable, which links the will of God with the will of man, in the decisive act which " binds " the "strong man " and yields an undivided allegiance to Christ.

Neither does conversion of this type mean that there will be no other conflicts with sin. Even in the case of Jesus, the Tempter only left Him " for a season." There will be other battles with temptation and sin in the Christian life, but the man, who by the help of Christ has once overcome, can have strength to overcome again. He who has walked in the light and liberty of Christ and has known His love, can never be like those who have not had these purifying and strengthening experiences. And He who first "bound" the "strong man " for us, and helped us to turn with an undivided will to Himself, will keep us stedfast to the end.

3. If it is the rule for the beginning of the Christian life that evil must be conquered in its seat of strength, it is also the rule for all effective service

of Christ in the world. All work for Christ must be done in His Spirit and in His way. If His triumphs were won by His absolute freedom from evil, the power of His followers to repeat His works will be in direct proportion to their possession of the same unworldly and spiritual quality. The " strong man " must be "bound " before his house can be spoiled. Personal victory over the strength of evil must be won, before any effectual help can be given to others who are under its power. The Christian character is the mightiest force for righteousness. It is not what we say or do that most influences others. It is from our character that our words and deeds get their power. Helpers of men must be assured that sin can be overcome, and no assurance is equal to that which comes from personal experience. Hearsay evidence will not serve. It may help, but it will not clothe with might. Is this the explanation of the comparative weakness of the Christian Church in face of the world's need to-day ? Are there traitors in the camp—men and women who own a divided allegiance ? Is it but " by parts " they " follow good or ill ? " Are they seeking to lead others to the Saviour, when they themselves are not the " redeemed of the Lord ? " There is no weaker power in God's world than an unholy Church. A holy Church will be " fair as the moon, clear as the

First Bind the Strong Man

sun, and terrible as an army with banners." Its power will be in direct proportion to its holiness. May we not say that " the earnest expectation of the creature waiteth for the manifestation of the children of God ? " The transmission of electric force depends on the perfection of the insulation of the wire by which it is conveyed. The transmission of the saving energies of Christ is in proportion to the Christian's deliverance from evil. The " strong man " must be " bound " before his house is spoiled.

Power in any sphere of moral action, depends upon our personal freedom from the evil against which we are contending. The ignorant will never succeed in enlightening the ignorant, nor the blind in leading the blind. We may set a thief to catch a thief, but never to reform him ! It is folly for a drunkard, or one who is in any way the slave, or even the servant, of strong drink, to attempt the reformation of the drunkard. If it is so in these spheres of moral endeavour, the principle holds as strongly in the more subtle conflicts with the power of sin in the soul. Nothing is more futile than for men and women, themselves unsaved, to engage in the work of saving others. They know not the glory and wonder of the power of Christ, and can only speak in hesitating accents to those whom they would lead to the Saviour.

The First Things of Jesus

Therefore, in every Christian life that is to be strong and helpful, there must be an experience similar to that of Jesus, when He " bound the strong man," and yielded up His life as a unity to the will of God. Utter consecration to Him has been the secret and strength of all who have wrought effectively for Him in the world. When Livingstone was found dead on his knees in a little hut in Central Africa, his diary was open before him, and its last entry was " Jesus, my Saviour, my Life, my All, anew I dedicate myself to Thee." This dying resolve casts an illuminating light on all the life that went before. It unveils the secret of his redeeming service in that darkened land. In an old museum in Germany there is a sword, on the blade of which the words are inscribed, " My value varies with the hand that holds me." The saying is true of the lives of men. Their value is in accordance with the Hand that rules their will and guides their actions. " Concentration," said Napoleon, " is the secret of victory," and what is consecration but the concentration of all the energies of life under the control of Christ ? " He that wavereth is like a wave of the sea, driven with the wind and tossed. Let not that man think that he will receive anything from the Lord," or do anything for Him. We cannot serve two masters. One alone must be chosen. A divided will is weakness.

Let the Children first be filled

" (In the forest) as elsewhere, the Unfulfilled Intention, which makes life what it is, was as obvious as it could be among the degraded crowds of a city slum. The leaf was deformed, the curve was crippled, the taper interrupted ; the lichen ate the vigour of the stalk, and the ivy slowly strangled to death the promising sapling."

THOMAS HARDY, *The Woodlanders.*

" But others hear a summons like a keen
    Bright sword, which thrills, and pierces and
        divides
Asunder joints and marrow."

MISS HICKEY, *Michael Villiers, Idealist.*

" Now is my soul troubled and what shall I say ? Father, save me from this hour. But for this cause came I unto this hour. Father glorify Thy Name."

OUR LORD JESUS.

CHAPTER II

" LET THE CHILDREN FIRST BE FILLED "

THE retreat of Jesus to the coasts of Tyre and Sidon was the occasion of the enunciation of one of the great ruling principles of His life. His ministry in Galilee had come to a crisis. If we read the story of the miracle of the feeding of the five thousand (Matt. xiv. 14-21), in conjunction with the account of what followed it in the Gospel according to John (chap. vi.), we see that the interpretation of the miracle, as symbolical of the Bread of Life, had given great offence. " From that time many of His disciples went back and walked no more with Him." The divergence between their views and His had become evident. Instead of desiring to make Him a king, the people would have nothing more to do with Him. The Pharisees, ready to take advantage of His unpopularity, sent to ask why His disciples disregarded the traditions about cleansing. His answer offended them also. Both people and rulers were hostile to Him. The death of John the Baptist, which had occurred shortly before, had also cast its ominous shadow over His spirit. Everything pointed to a change in the conditions of His ministry, and to the possibility of His ultimate rejection. The crisis forced upon Jesus the necessity of reconsidering the plan of His life work. Rest and seclusion were necessary, that He might have time for thought on the new situation. Now, for the first time, the Cross came clearly into the view of the future. We notice that it was after His return from the borders of Tyre and Sidon, that He conferred with Moses and Elias about " the exodus He was to accomplish at Jerusalem," and began to speak " openly " to His disciples about His death. It was in the quiet and loneliness of the borders of a heathen land that Jesus grappled with the questions which arose out of the crisis which His ministry had reached ; it was there that He determined to endure the Cross, and give His life a ransom for many. The withdrawal to the coasts of Tyre and Sidon had the same end in view as when He was driven into the Wilderness to be tempted of the devil. He must settle the way which He was to take in the fulfilment of His mission.

1. " He would have no man know " where He was, " but He could not be hid " (Mark vii. 24). The fame of His works had spread far beyond the districts in which they had been wrought. The

Let the Children first be filled

story of His merciful kindness had been heard by a Gentile mother. The memory of it stirred in her heart as she watched beside her little daughter. She acted instantly when she heard that the famous Healer had come near to the place where she lived. With all the eagerness of a mother's loving anxiety, she sought Him out and poured forth her prayer, " Have mercy upon me, O Lord, Thou Son of David ; my daughter is grievously vexed with a demon " (Matt. xv. 22).

But she had a chilling reception. The kind and compassionate Healer did not seem to live up to His reputation. " He answered her not a word." The disciples appear to have been surprised at their Master's silence. He was acting as He had never acted before.   His silence was not a momentary pause ; it lasted so long that the disciples could not bear it. They must break it, if He did not. So they came and begged Him to send her away. But that was what He did not do ; what we believe He could not do.   He spoke at last in words which seem to express a conclusion to which He had come in the silence—" Let the children first be filled ; I am not sent but unto the lost sheep of the house of Israel ; it is not meet to take the children's bread and cast it to the dogs " (Matt. xv. 24-26 ; Mark vii. 27). The words have a harsher sound in English than in Greek, for it is the diminutive which is used—" little dogs," the pets of the household. They may not have struck so rudely on her ears as they do on ours, for we cannot reproduce the tone in which they were spoken. Possibly the phrase about the dogs was a proverb of the time, and the woman's answer looks like its companion, " Yea, Lord, yet the little dogs under the table eat of the children's crumbs." Proverbs often go in pairs, and it may have been so on this occasion.*   At any rate, the seemingly contemptuous words did not drive her away. Perhaps the sorrow in her own heart enabled her to recognise that there was a secret sorrow in His. She may have seen that it was something else than want of will that restrained His kindliness. She persisted in her importunity, and her faith and mother-wit gained for her the boon she craved. A gracious word sent her home rejoicing—" O woman, great is thy faith ; be it unto thee even as thou wilt."

It is our Lord's silence and reluctance to grant at once this woman's prayer which is the chief problem. It contradicts the outstanding characteristic of His whole ministry. It presents Him in an attitude which is entirely unexpected. Never before did He refuse a suppliant. Even when admiring crowds attempted to silence the clamorous cries of Bartimæus, He said, " Bring him to Me."

* Rev. David Smith, D.D. " In the Days of His Flesh," p. 251.

Let the Children first be filled

How is His reluctance in this instance to be explained ? There were no racial or geographical limits to His sympathies. He was as keenly touched by the need of the Gentile woman as He was by that of any mother in Israel, yet, for the first and only time in His life, an appeal was made to Him on behalf of a sufferer—on behalf of a suffering child, and by a loving mother— and it was received in silence. It is this surprising contradiction which constitutes the difficulty of this incident.

2. We set aside as unsatisfactory all the explanations which are based on the particular words used by the woman in addressing Jesus, or on her supposed spiritual condition. We also set aside the suppositions of consideration on the part of Jesus for the prejudices of the Jews, or of His desire to educate His disciples out of their national narrowness. Consideration for the prejudices of the Jews never affected His actions. Their antipathy to the Samaritans did not hinder Him from doing kindness to them, or from praising them for their excellences. We cannot imagine that Jesus would vivisect the anguished heart of a mother to show to His disciples the kind of conduct that their narrow notions would produce. Further, it is exceedingly difficult to think that our Lord kept silence because the poor woman had addressed Him as " Son of David "

—a title to which, as a Gentile, she had no right. Is it Christ-like to listen in silence to the anguished cry of a mother's heart, or to speak words of contempt to her because, forsooth, she had not used the proper form of words in her prayer ? Then, as to the need of educating her faith, this woman seems to have had more of it than most of those on whom works of healing were wrought. Jesus was surprised at the greatness of it, and gave her such praise as He never gave to a disciple. These methods of accounting for the Lord's behaviour at this time are all futile and needless. He Himself gives the reasons for His surprising conduct. " Let the children first be filled ; I am not sent but unto the lost sheep of the house of Israel ; it is not meet to take the children's bread and cast it unto dogs." It is in these words that we must seek the solution of the problem which His silence and reluctance have raised. Their significance may be more fully recognised if they are carefully weighed, and examined in relation to the crisis which had arisen in the ministry of Jesus, the pressure of which had driven Him into the coasts of Tyre and Sidon.

3. The answer of Jesus is a carefully considered utterance. It was spoken after a long and embarrassing silence. It was a conclusion which He had reached while He held His peace. It seems to refer to a much larger question than that which

Let the Children first be filled

was suggested by the prayer of the woman. The
" children's bread " would not be exhausted, or
its supply endangered by anything that might be
given to this single applicant. Then, it was not
" bread " which was sought, but healing. The
use of the word " bread " is a hitherto unnoticed
link, that recalls the explanation of the miracle
of the feeding of the five thousand, which had been
given immediately before Jesus left Galilee for the
borders of Tyre and Sidon. It refers to Himself, for
He is the " Bread of Life " and the " Children's
Bread." The lost sheep of the house of Israel
would not miss any part of the blessing which was
reserved for them, by the healing of one Gentile
child, as they had not suffered any loss through
the healing of the centurion's servant in Capernaum.
From the words of His answer, it is evident that
there was another and a larger matter before His
mind than the particular plea which the woman
presented.

We must recall the fact that it was a crisis in
His ministry which had led Him to seek seclusion
in that particular neighbourhood. His popularity
in Galilee had declined ; the hostility of the Pharisees
had become more intense and deadly. A tragic
end to His life was now clearly foreshadowed.
His ministry must now be carried on in new conditions. But it was not intense absorption in the

consideration of these things which kept Him silent when the cry of the woman broke in upon His seclusion. He who at the moment of His arrest in the Garden of Gethsemane cared for the safety of His disciples, and healed the ear of Malchus ; who on the Cross remembered the need of His mother, and answered the prayer of the dying robber, could never be so self-absorbed in His own interests and anxieties that He could not hear the cry of a loving mother's anguish. More likely His silence was caused by the sudden emergence of a great question which had never been clearly present to His mind before—a question which the cry of the woman combined with His own circumstances had suggested—the possibility of a personal mission to the Gentile world. He had been rejected or at least forsaken by His own countrymen, and would be put to death if He returned to them. Here at His feet was the proof that He was needed and desired by the Gentiles. Was this woman's approach to Him a leading of the Heavenly Father ?* Was it a sign that He was to leave those who would not receive Him and betake Himself to those who desired Him ? Should He give Himself, " the Bread of Life," to the Gentiles ? May His soul not have been troubled now as it was at a

* Suggested by the late Prof. A. B. Bruce, D.D. "Expositor." Fifth Series, vol. iv., p. 38.

Let the Children first be filled

later time, when the Greeks came desiring to see Him (John xii. 20-27) ? The case of the Gentile centurion in Capernaum, whose servant He healed, did not suggest the possibility of a ministry to the Gentiles. There was no likelihood that He would be drawn to devote Himself to them at that time, or by that act of kindness. But here on the borders of the Gentile world, with unbelieving Jews behind Him, and the anxious woman before Him, the idea may have flashed across His mind, that work among the Gentiles was a possibility, perhaps even the will of God. The world-wide scope of His mission was clear to Him from the beginning—it was no afterthought to Him or His disciples—but was He Himself to take no part in it ? How He must have longed to do something for the great world lying in darkness !

4. It may have been His preoccupation with this question which kept Him silent so long. But we think that there was another thought mingling with it, which accounts not only for His silence, but for the harshness and severity of His words to the woman. It was, we believe, while on the borders of Tyre and Sidon that the thought of the Cross came clearly to His mind. The idea of the artist in the picture of " The Shadow of the Cross," however true it may seem to us looking back over the whole of the life of Jesus, was not

true to Him. The "shadow" crept over Him gradually. There had been partial glimpses of it before, but in this time of seclusion the Cross stood out "against the sky" terrible in its inevitableness. From this period it formed part of His consciousness. May not the approach of this woman have been the occasion of an unnoticed temptation ? If He were to cross the borders into the Gentile world, might He not labour among the heathen, telling them of the Kingdom of God, and the love of the Heavenly Father whom they did not know, after whom they were dimly seeking ? He could do among them all that He had done in Israel, teaching, healing, showing mercy, bringing light to their darkened lives. He could break among them the " Bread of Life " *and avoid the Cross*. That possibility was the temptation which came to Him in the loving remonstrance of St. Peter (Matt. xvi. 22). It may have come to Him now in the cry of the woman. She was uttering the prayer of the vast waiting multitudes, who had not even the language of a cry. The natural shrinking from the Cross, and the suggestion of an honourable way of escape from it through a ministry to the Gentiles, may have created a spiritual conflict in the mind of Jesus which kept Him silent until it was ended. The intensity of the struggle may have imparted the tone of severity which rings through His words.

Let the Children first be filled

He was deeply moved when St. Peter took Him aside and began to rebuke Him. He addressed to him the sternest word He ever spoke to a disciple— He said : " Get thee behind Me, Satan." It was the power of the temptation which made Him answer in this way the loving anxiety of the Apostle. The same feelings may have moved Him when He replied to the prayer of the woman in the forbidding words, " Let the children first be filled ; it is not meet to take the children's bread and cast it unto the dogs." The harshness of tone in both cases may have sprung from the same source—the intensity of His emotion under a strong temptation. We feel that He was not only answering the woman, but repelling the attractions of the possibilities which lay in a ministry among the Gentiles. Through the stress of a great spiritual conflict, He definitely turned from the way of escape. He could not take the " children's bread " and give it to the Gentiles. He must limit Himself to the lost sheep of the house of Israel.

In determining and expressing this principle of His ministry there was in Him no sympathy with Jewish prejudice, no contempt for Gentiles. For His work's sake He must limit Himself to the Jews ; must once appear as if He shared in their narrowness ; must discourage the appeals which the Gentiles would only be too ready to make to Him. The way of the Cross was not to be shunned, however hard it might be, or however tempting the way of escape. The boon which was sought by the Gentile mother was granted, but in such a way that it would not interfere with the great plan of His mission. For the sake of it He must confine Himself to the lost sheep of the house of Israel. A personal ministry among the Gentiles was impossible. The day of the Gentiles was coming, but the deep darkness of the Cross had to pass before it could dawn. Jesus had come to see that only by suffering and death could He finish the work which had been given Him to do. The Messiah without the Cross would be destitute of His power and glory. Only when " lifted up " would He " draw all men unto Him." The law of the Kingdom of God which He was to establish demanded sacrifice —a sacrifice crowned by the Cross—and He would not shrink from it.

5. We can easily see other reasons for the decision of Jesus to hold to His ministry among the Jews. He must have respect to the past dealings of God with the chosen people. He could not set aside as unimportant the discipline of preparation through which they had passed. The progress of revelation which had been advancing from the days of Abraham must be continued and completed. The promises of type and prophecy had

Let the Children first be filled

to be fulfilled. The Jews had been unfaithful to their privileges, but their unbelief did not make the promises of God of none effect. The faithfulness of God was involved in the steadfastness of Jesus to His mission among them, even though they rejected Him, as they had rejected those who had spoken of His coming. In this matter Jesus was as " a man under authority." He could not alter the terms of His commission. He must confine Himself to a ministry among them," whether they would hear or whether they would forbear." He knew too well the tendency of the stream of Promise to think of changing its direction. He turned from the tempting way of a ministry among the Gentiles, with the declaration of the limits of His personal mission—" I am not sent but unto the lost sheep of the house of Israel."

Then, also, in the crisis of His ministry He now read with clearer understanding the prophecies of suffering and sacrifice which ran like a crimson thread through the Scriptures. He expounded to Himself in all the Scriptures the things concerning Himself. Soon He would talk with Moses and Elias about the decease He was to accomplish at Jerusalem, and speak " openly " to His disciples about it. But where could the prophecies be fulfilled which spoke of the suffering of the Messiah and the glory that should follow ? He must needs walk " to-day and to-morrow, and the day following, for it cannot be that a prophet perish out of Jerusalem." Where also could the redemptive significance of His sacrifice be understood ? Who of the Gentiles would be able to read its meaning, without the clue which the Jews all unknown to themselves possessed ? Since the law of the Kingdom of God, and the redemptive will of His Father, involved the giving up of life in willing sacrifice, He must continue His ministry until the end among the lost sheep of the house of Israel. Otherwise God's great " intention " would have been " unfulfilled." Work among Gentiles did not provide the conditions in which His mission could be accomplished. To labour among them would be like beginning to build upon the bare ground. An entirely new foundation for the Kingdom of God would require to be laid, and it would lack its crown because it lacked the Cross. The Jews alone provided the conditions in which He could accomplish what He had been sent to do.

He knew well that the blessings which He was bringing were not for Jews only. All through His ministry the universal note is heard, and glimpses of the wider field are seen. But there is an order in the progress of the grace of God. To the " Jew first " must the blessing come, that through them " all the families of the earth might be blessed."

Let the Children first be filled

As He took the twelve apart that He might make them His missionaries to the Jews, so He looked upon the Jews as those who would be the missionaries to the world. Jesus recognised the law that rules in all the labours of mankind. There must be limitation that there may be expansion. Many things desirable and good in themselves must be set aside, because they are not the essential things, or because their time is not yet come. Energy would be dissipated if an attempt were made too soon to bring to the Gentiles the good news of the Gospel. There is no escape from this law of limitation, not even for the Son of God. The stream which is unconfined and wanders everywhere creates a marsh ; the stream which runs in channels becomes a river of the water of life wherever it goes. He who attempts too much accomplishes nothing permanent or fruitful ; he who limits himself to supreme duties becomes a benefactor of mankind.

The problem of the Gentile world is with us still. The call of the heathen is sounding in the ear of the churches. The Master's word says, " Go ye into all the world and preach the Gospel to every creature." Why is it that the call remains so largely unheeded ? Why are there so few, comparatively speaking, fulfilling the Master's will ? The time of limitation which confined the personal ministry of Jesus to one land is gone by. Yet may it not be that the law which Jesus obeyed is a law to which we must still give heed ? The evangelisation of the heathen is not to be measured by the numbers of those who are in the field or by those devoted Christians who are ready to go. It is the churches which must be made missionary in character and spirit. Those who labour in the Gospel at home, and feel the call of the heathen, need not always think that they are unfaithful when they are compelled by many reasons to stay at home. There are " lost sheep " to be gathered in, and above all there is the preparation of the Church for the missionary duty. Not till the whole Church receives the universal spirit of her Lord will the evangelisation of the heathen be attempted in a measure proportionate to the need.

The Son of Man must first Suffer

" The path of duty was the way to glory."
TENNYSON.

" Do not be afraid of anything ; neither the bitterest sorrow that the world holds, nor its most poignant joy, can bring you anything but good, so long as you embrace it willingly."
E. F. BENSON, *The Challoners*.

" In Khartoum a fine statue of General Gordon has been erected. He is seated on a dromedary with his face set towards the vast desert of the Soudan. It is said that a traveller asked a guide if the statue should not have been turned to face the city. ' O, no, sir,' was the reply, ' they set him not looking towards the palace where he lived, not towards the Nile by which he might have escaped, but towards the Soudan for which he died, and he is waiting, sir, for the morning to dawn over the Soudan.' "—HENRY C. MABIE, *The Message of the Cross*.

" The death of Christ was a blow that broke the alabaster box and set free the divine perfume of His heart, which was renunciation, sacrifice, love ! "
SABATIER.

CHAPTER III

"THE SON OF MAN . . . MUST FIRST SUFFER"

No one can read the New Testament with the slightest care without being struck by the remarkable prominence which it gives to the sufferings and death of Christ. A very large section of the Gospels is taken up with the record of the closing experiences of His life. In the Epistles, it is the importance and significance of these facts which are most strongly emphasised. It may be said that they are the chief subject of the thought of the Apostles and of the Apostolic writers. St. Paul is speaking for his brethren when he says, " I delivered unto you first of all that which I also received, how that Christ died for our sins according to the Scriptures " (1 Cor. xv. 3). It has been suggested that their absorbing interest in this matter was due to the fact, that they felt themselves under the necessity of giving an explanation of the disgraceful death of their Lord that would remove the horror and suspicion which it had naturally created. Such a suggestion can only be made by those who have set aside the Gospels as trustworthy records of the life and sayings of Jesus. To unbiassed readers, the references which Jesus is reported to have made to His sufferings and death are too numerous, and too closely interwoven with the texture of His teaching, to be accounted for in this hypothetical fashion. The supposition creates a more difficult problem than the fact. It makes the disciples greater than the Master, and endows them with a vision which is denied to Him.

1. The time when He began to tell His disciples that He must die is definitely marked, and its lateness is easily explained. It introduces the last stage of His ministry. There may have been hidden allusions to the tragic end at earlier times, as when He said about His disciples, " The days will come when the bridegroom shall be taken away from them, and then shall they fast in those days." But it is only after the Transfiguration, and the great confession of the disciples regarding His Messiahship, that He began to speak to them " openly " and frequently, about the way of pain and death which He must tread. It was only then that the disciples were ready, in the most imperfect way, to receive the first hints of this mystery. Even as it was, the revelation came almost too soon. It is a reasonable conclusion that the importance which is given to His death by the Apostles, is a conse-

quence of the personal teaching of Jesus. It became of great moment to them, because it was of great moment to Him.

For one thing it was absolutely unique among the religious conceptions of the world. We search the records and beliefs of other religions in vain, for any doctrine of redemption by the death of their originators. In Christianity alone is the healing of the world linked indissolubly with the personal suffering and death of its Founder. It is a new departure, the introduction of a hitherto unknown conception. An idea which is peculiar to the religion of Christ, which distinguishes it from other faiths, cannot be an invention or an afterthought of His disciples. It can only have come from Christ Himself.

2. Further, in speaking of His sufferings and death, Jesus was running counter to the general expectations of the time. The idea of a suffering Messiah was scarcely in existence among the Jews. The Messiah was to be a Prince, who should come in great power and glory. The disciples evidently shared in the beliefs of the people. The lowliness of their Master's life was a perplexity to them. They wondered how it was that He did not manifest Himself to the world as He did to them. His humility was a veil which was soon to be thrown aside ; then the glory of the Messiah would be

revealed, the Kingdom of God would come, and they would hold the first places in it. Jerusalem would become the metropolis of the world, and abundant prosperity would gladden and enrich the Jews. It never dawned upon their minds that the Messiah was to die in shame and pain, or that He would reach His glory through His sufferings. They could not have originated this peculiar idea. When it was first plainly intimated to them, they received the announcement with the utmost repugnance. Peter took His Master aside, and began to rebuke Him. He cried, " Lord, that be far from Thee ; this shall not be unto Thee." They shrank in dismay and horror from the prospect which the words of Jesus called up before them. The way of the Cross was unthinkable to them. It was not only the destruction of the hopes which they cherished for themselves and for Israel, but it was a fate which they could not bear to imagine as overtaking the Master whom they loved. The prophecy was so alien to their thoughts that they could scarcely receive it. The startling news made no abiding impression upon their minds. Even when Jesus again assured them that for Him an early and violent death was inevitable, they so little realised the truth of what He said, that they still continued to cherish dreams of worldly greatness, and were ready to quarrel about their conflicting ambitions.

The Son of Man must first Suffer

There is no rational possibility that these men could originate a belief which was so diametrically opposed to all their fondly cherished hopes. The idea that the sufferings and death of Jesus were redemptive forces can only be attributed to the definite teaching of Jesus. It was He alone who foresaw how the Messiah would enter into His glory. He sought to prepare the disciples for the tragedy of His death, and to give them a clue to its significance. The time when it would take place was in the hand of God. It would come with His own " hour."

3. The prophetic announcement or knowledge of the fate which awaited Jesus is not a perplexity or a problem. Apart from His own experience of the opposition and hatred of the Pharisees, which had been growing in strength and virulence, and must continue to grow, He had the history of the prophets to guide Him. Their fate as preachers of righteousness was certain to be His fate. His foes were the children of those who had slain the prophets, and they would be true to their descent. What the fathers had done to the prophets, the sons would do to Him. He had no need to wait till their hatred had reached its height. He could see the course which it would take, long before it had attained its strength. His condemnation of their unrighteousness ; His exposure of their hypocrisy ;

The First Things of Jesus

His disregard of their cherished traditions ; His
contempt of their treasured customs, could not be
recalled or altered. The opposition between their
ideal of goodness and His could not be lessened.
Faithfulness to the conceptions of right which
possessed Him must be continued, and as the hope
of repentance on their part was not to be looked
for, there was nothing in prospect but growing
estrangement, more bitter hatred, more intense
hostility. Even Plato could foresee the end which
awaited " a man of true simplicity and nobleness,
who had resolved not to seem but to be good "—
" who without being guilty of one unjust act, shall
have the worst reputation for injustice,"—" who
goes on till the day of his death, steadfast in his
justice, but with a lifelong reputation for injustice "
—" the just man will be scourged, racked and
fettered, will have his eyes burnt out, and at last,
after suffering every kind of torture, will be
crucified."* If we translate the Greek words " just,"
" justice " and " injustice " in this passage by the
Biblical terms " righteous," " righteousness " and
" unrighteousness," the forecast of Plato is a
prophecy, which in its main outlines corresponds
with the experience of Jesus. The words " will
be crucified " startle us with the surprise of their
truth. They are one of the most remarkable

* " Republic," Book ii., pp. 46, 47 (Golden Treasury Edition).

approaches of the thought of Greece to the life-experience of Jesus.

4. But it is not the forecast of a violent death which constitutes the problem for the student of the death of Jesus. It is the significance which Jesus attaches to it. The death was a martyrdom, a consequence of His faithfulness to right and truth, but it was more. Its inevitableness did not arise because He would not swerve from the straight path which He was treading, and thus avoid collision with the forces of evil. It was inevitable, because only by its means could the work of the Messiah be accomplished. " The Son of Man . . . must first suffer many things " (Luke xvii. 24-25), before He could bring in the Kingdom of God, and work out redemption for sinners. The peculiarity of the thought of Jesus is that it was not by His words of revelation, or His deeds of mercy, or His life of love, but by His sufferings and death, that He was to be the Saviour of men. His death was not simply a cruel tragedy, by which the Pharisees brought His ministry to an end ; it was the means by which His redemptive mission was fulfilled. It is the paradox of Christianity. What the disciples regarded as an unspeakable and overwhelming tragedy, what the rulers planned as the final and certain method of ridding the world of the " troubler of Israel," what the world in its wisdom has called

The First Things of Jesus

" foolishness," was to Jesus the way in which He completed the work which had been given Him to do. It is our familiarity with the doctrine which hides from us the uniqueness of this fact. It is a " stupendous originality,"* the wonder of the ages, that life should spring through death, that pardon and reconciliation, and all the grace of redeeming love, should come through the death of the Son of Man. Nowhere else is this idea to be found, except in the faith which Jesus gave to the world. In the whole range of religious literature, the blessings which have been brought by the leaders and deliverers of men are the results of their teaching and example, never of their suffering and death. It was Jesus who first revealed the truth and reality of the divine possibilities of death, and its might as a redeeming power. He first saw that the law of fruitfulness in the sphere of nature held good in the realm of spirit, that " except a corn of wheat fall into the ground and die, it abideth alone, but if it die it bringeth forth much fruit " (John xii. 24). A glimmer of the idea, as working in a lower sphere, came to Caiaphas, " he being the high-priest that same year," when he said, " It is expedient for us that one man die for the people, and that the whole nation perish not " (John xi. 50). He did not know that Jesus died " not for that nation only,

* Principal Fairbairn.

The Son of Man must first Suffer

but that He also should gather together in one the children of God that were scattered abroad" (John xi. 52). When we say that the "blood of the martyrs is the seed of the Church" we are interpreting martyrdom in the light of the revelation which Jesus gave when He said "the Son of Man must first suffer many things." Even yet the idea is so amazing that we have cause to say—

> "Is it not strange, the darkest hour
>   That ever dawned on mortal earth
> Should touch the heart with softer power
>   For comfort than an angel's mirth;
> That to the Cross the mourner's eye should turn
> Sooner than where the stars of Christmas burn?"*

The doctrine of the Cross must ever be essential to any true exposition of Christianity. Because it is peculiar, it must be central and distinctive. There is no Christianity without it. The Temptation in the Wilderness and the remonstrance of Peter were inspired by the worldly conception that the work of the Messiah could be done apart from suffering and death.

The inability of the disciples to enter into the thought of Jesus explains why He said so little to them about the significance of His death. As they could not accept the fact, it was useless to attempt its interpretation. He could only give

* Keble, " Christian Year," *Good Friday.*

them hints and symbols of its meaning, leaving it to the influence of the promised Spirit to guide them into the truth, when once the prophecy of death was accomplished. Many things which He did and said " the disciples understood not at the first." His death was the chief of these. In the Acts of the Apostles and the Epistles, we have the record of their understanding of the mystery which had overwhelmed them, as it was unfolded to them under the guidance of the Holy Spirit. It is there that we must look for the ruling interpretations of its worth and efficacy. Not even yet can the followers of Christ dispense with the help of that Guide. The mystery of the Cross has not yet been solved. After all the thought and effort of the Christian centuries, its significance is not yet fully known. New light is still to break forth from it upon the darkened ways of men. Into its secret we still desire to look, that we may know more of its wonder and power.

5. Of the hints and symbols which Jesus gave the most striking is expressed in the words " The Son of Man came . . . to give His life a ransom for many " (Matt. xx. 28). His death was not an experience through which He had to pass because He was made in the likeness of men, and shared in the mortality which is inherent in their nature. It was the experience of the Messiah, the suffering which was bound up with the work He had come

to do. Death was in His " cup "; it was the " baptism " wherewith He was to be baptised. The way of service which the Son of Man had followed in the years of His ministry led Him to the heights of sacrifice. He must obey the law of the Kingdom of God which He was to establish. Not by worldly power or might, but by the ministry of love ; not by self-seeking, but by self-sacrifice, was He to reach the throne of His glory. The " Son of Man must go as it had been determined," but the necessity was laid upon Him by the methods and aims of the Messiah-ship.

The death was not a fate to which He submitted but a sacrifice which He offered. He " gave His life a ransom for many." His life was not taken ; it was given. He was led as a lamb to the slaughter, but He went voluntarily. Beyond the hatred of men He saw the loving purpose of God ; beyond the gloom and shame of the Cross He saw the deliverance of " many." It was to that gracious will of His Heavenly Father, and to that glorious end, that He bowed Himself in ready obedience. To the hero in *Prometheus Vinctus*, bound in chains and the prey of the vulture, it was said " Expect not any termination to thine anguish, till some one of the gods appear as thy successor, and be willing to go down into the unlighted Hades, and around the gloomy depths of Tartarus." But, to Æschylus, that was merely a rhetorical way of saying that deliverance was impossible. But what to the wisdom of the Greeks was impossible, was an unconscious prophecy of that which was possible with God. One of the gods, if we may so speak, has appeared, and has been willing to go down to all depths, that the captives bound in the chains of sin might be released. The old cry of the servant of God was fulfilled in Jesus, " Lo, I come, in the volume of the book it is written of me, I delight to do Thy will, O my God " (Psalm xl. 7, 8). It is the willingness of love which gives obedience its peculiar efficacy. Suffering in itself has no redeeming power ; the endurance of it is not necessarily sacrificial or beneficial. It may be degrading, if it is borne for selfish or cowardly reasons. It ennobles and redeems only when it is endured for love's sake. To suffer willingly, that good may come, is a proof of love which few can resist. It is the motive and spirit of Jesus which gives to His death its redemptive might.

He speaks of His sacrifice as a " ransom "— the price paid for deliverance. He does not expound the figure, and care must be taken lest its suggestions are followed too particularly. There is no place in its interpretation for pedantic questions, as to whom the ransom was paid, or what was the precise equivalent which it was to secure. It is the

The Son of Man must first Suffer

broad and general meaning of the figure which is to be emphasised. It is to be treated as a spiritual symbol, not as a legal or theological term. Its connection with His explanation of the secret of greatness in the Kingdom of God (Matt. xx. 20-28) is the clue which must be followed as we seek to grasp its significance. His methods of service and sacrifice are illustrations of the law and life of the Kingdom of God, and are examples for the guidance of His followers. They are to be " even as the Son of Man," who " came not to be ministered unto but to minister, and to give His life a ransom for many." He does not say that, by obedience to the law of the Kingdom, the lives of His followers will have the power of a ransom, though in measure that is true. We must not quote the cry of the Old Testament and say, " None can redeem his brother, or give to God a ransom for him," as if it denied to man all share in the power that is in the death of Jesus. That saying referred to redemption from the power of the grave, and was spoken before the Saviour had revealed the possibilities of unselfish suffering and loving sacrifice to deliver from the power of sin. Yet when we compare the strength and power of the ransom which He made, there is none to stand beside it. It is His obedience only which has gathered to itself the fulness of this liberating efficacy. Other effects it also has which we find set forth in the thoughts of His servants, as the Holy Spirit led them into all the truth. But He limits Himself here to one result of His Passion. It acts like a ransom, it is a means of deliverance. How it acts in this way He does not say, and we can only dimly trace the workings of its power. But this we know assuredly, that it has been even as He said. The sacrifice which was to the disciples the tragedy of tragedies, has become the means of the redemption of the world. The love that stooped to death has brought life to the dead, hope to the despairing, freedom to the enslaved, the assurance of the reality of the love of God to a loveless world. The forgiveness, which triumphed over the experience of the worst that the cruelty and malice of men could inflict, that prayed, " Father forgive them for they know not what they do," shines like the sun in the skies, revealing the unfathomed grace of the heart of God, and quickening penitence and the longing for pardon and reconciliation in sin-bound souls. For it is in the chains of sin, and unbelief, and fear, that men are bound, and it is from these prisons of the soul that Jesus ransoms them.

The same thoughts underlie the mystic words, in which He referred to His death at the institution of the Supper. " This is My blood of the New Covenant which is shed for many, for the remission of sins " (Matt. xxvi. 28). Here the effect is the same, for remission means deliverance, the letting go of something by which men were bound. It is the forgiveness of sins. But the death of Christ in this passage is more than a ransom. The " remission of sins " through the outpoured blood of the Son of Man is linked with the types and sacrifices of the Old Covenant. We think of the Paschal Lamb, the peace-offering, the sin-offering, with all their typical and prophetic meaning. It is a self-offering of life in love, fulfilling them all, introducing and sealing a New Covenant. It has influence not only on the heart of man as a revelation of unspeakable love, but in that unexplored region of the righteousness and law of God, of which it is the great essential principle that " without shedding of blood there is no remission."

Here, also, as in the other passage, the blessing which the death of Christ secures is for " many." The word is not to be taken in any exclusive sense. It stands as an indication of the largeness of the result, of the wide scope and action of the ransoming and redeeming power of the sacrifice of the Son of Man. The contrast lies between the death of One and the vastness of the number of those for whom it avails. Death was not a failure to Him, or the ending or lessening of His power and influence. It was the means by which the fountain of

The First Things of Jesus

His might was broken up, that the streams of His grace might flow forth in all their fulness. The " many " loom in large outline—they are the " multitude which no man can number," who are the fruit of the travail of His soul, the justification of His devotion, the joy that was set before Him when He endured the Cross, despising the shame.

In these days, it is sometimes said that the preaching of the Cross is futile, a needless encumbrance to the might of the pure morality of Jesus. Men say, Preach the Fatherhood of God and the Brotherhood of Man ; expound the morals of Jesus ; set His example before us, and teach us how to follow it, but let us hear nothing of the mystery of His sufferings and death. It is still a " folly " to the world. But it is the essence of the Gospel, according to the mind of Christ. These modern counsellors of preachers forget that the words of Jesus regarding the Fatherhood of God and the Brotherhood of Man ; the works of Jesus in all the might of their mercy and helpfulness ; the example of Jesus with all the grace of its actual presence in the world, were tried in His lifetime, and that the men of His time cried " Away with Him!" It is not by His teaching or example that the faith of Jesus has won its victories in the world. It is by the Cross. He said, " I, if I be lifted up, will draw all men unto Me." He " reigns from the Tree."

The Son of Man must first Suffer

We are not to set the death of Christ apart from the life of Christ, or regard His death as the sole saving means, or think that His life had no redemptive influence. His life and death are one; both are redemptive. But it is in the death of Christ that the redemptive forces of His love are concentrated. We may say that His life was " a " power, but His death was " the " power of God unto salvation to everyone that believeth. There the Fatherhood of God is seen in its highest, the Brotherhood of men in its widest, the mercy and love of Christ in their fullest measure. Therefore through faith and experience we say with St. Paul, " God forbid that I should glory, save in the Cross of our Lord Jesus Christ, by whom the world is crucified unto me and I unto the world!"

The Gospel must first be Preached among all Nations

" The age of revolution has always been preceded
by the doctrinaire age ; the teachers to-day, the
actors to-morrow ; Christ and His Apostles to-day,
and a Christianised Europe to-morrow ; Luther and
Erasmus to-day, and the Reformation to-morrow ;
Diderot, Helvetius and Reynal to-day, and the
French Revolution to-morrow."

BOYD CARPENTER, *Permanent Elements of Religion.*

" The luxurious Babylonians were destroyed by
the frugal Persians ; the Persians, having learned the
vices of prosperity, were put to the sword by the
Greeks ; the Greeks when they became sensual were
trodden down by the robust and hardy Romans ; and
the Romans having lost their manly virtues, were
subdued by the nations of the North. Vice and
destruction come ever hand in hand."

CONAN DOYLE, *Micah Clarke.*

" When men are ripe for slaughter, even straws
become thunderbolts."—*Hindu Saying.*

CHAPTER IV

"THE GOSPEL MUST FIRST BE PREACHED AMONG ALL
NATIONS"

THE eschatological discourses of our Lord in the closing chapters of the Synoptic Gospels are a constant perplexity to the student of His words. They are like a great and gloomy forest through which no clear pathway has been found ; a labyrinth to which we have no certain clue. They loom before us, terrible in their suggestions of mystery and judgment. He who attempts to make a way through them has to walk in the dark, or at best in the gloom, and will always speak with modesty as to the finality of the line of interpretation which he may adopt.

Our special object in this study is to discover the place which the preaching of the Gospel had in our Lord's forecast of the end. Before we can do so, we must understand something of the character of the discourses in which the statement appears —that " the Gospel must first be preached among all nations " (Mark xiii. 10).

The First Things of Jesus

1. However mysterious these fateful utterances may be, certain facts are now generally admitted regarding them. It is recognised that they belong to a type of literature which is called apocalyptic. Though not confined to Jewish authors, it was most largely used by them. Its form and language are very strange to us. It is a mode of utterance which was used by prophets, in certain definite circumstances, to give expression to the vision with which they were burdened. The book of Daniel and parts of the book of Joel are specimens of this type of literature in the Old Testament. The book of Revelation and the discourses of our Lord in the last chapters of the Synoptic Gospels are the chief illustrations of it in the New Testament. Outside the Bible we have the Apocalypses of Enoch, of Baruch, of Esdras, etc.

The circumstances in which apocalypses appeared are always in broad outline the same. They are a product of crisis in national history, or of overwhelming calamity in the state. The tribulation which the prophet saw or foresaw is set forth in imagery drawn from descriptions of vast and terrible natural convulsions. The crisis or calamity is always interpreted under the law of righteousness ; and appropriate counsels, warnings, and promises are linked with the prophetic announcement. In every case the idea of judgment is strongly emphasised,

The Gospel must first be Preached

and the triumph of righteousness is the invariable conclusion in which the whole majestic progress of the apocalyptic drama ends. Then, without any definite break in the narrative, the prophet usually passes from the announcement of the national judgment, to a description of the end of the world, as if it lay immediately beyond the particular catastrophe with which he is dealing. In some cases the final judgment is so closely connected with the particular judgment out of which the thought of it sprang, that there is no clear separation of the one from the other in the prophetic utterance. The prophet sees the judgment of a nation in connection with the " great event to which the whole creation moves," and speaks of it as if it were the beginning, or herald, of that awful climax in the world's history. In the book of Joel, for example, the calamity of the plague of locusts merges imperceptibly into a description of the " great and terrible Day of the Lord." The Day is an emphatic symbol of the ultimate and irresistible triumph of righteousness. It matters not how dark the prospect is, the vindication and the victory of righteousness are absolutely sure.

2. The apocalyptic utterances of our Lord are to be read and interpreted in the same way as other instances of this kind of literature.* The particular

* Winterbotham, "Expositor," Sixth Series, vol. ii, pp. 405 ff.

crisis which He foresaw was the destruction of Jerusalem. The signs of the coming of that great disaster were wars, famines, pestilences, earthquakes, and persecutions. The *débacle* of the Jewish state culminates in the coming of the Son of Man. It is the symbol of His triumph. The Parousia of the Son of Man, as in the apocalypse of Daniel, takes the place of the " Day of the Lord." Then, " immediately after the tribulation of these days," the usual apocalyptic signs are to appear in the skies —" the sun shall be darkened, and the moon shall not give her light ; the stars shall fall from heaven, and the powers of the heaven shall be shaken " (Matt. xxiv. 29). The judgment of the Jewish state has merged into the judgment of the world. At times it is difficult, if not impossible, to distinguish between what belongs to the description of the one event and what to the other. The terrifying phenomena of the skies are followed by the sign of the Son of Man, and He Himself is to come in the clouds of heaven with power and great glory, for the awful and final judgment of mankind. There is no indication in His utterances, any more than in those of Joel, that there is any interval between the judgment of Jerusalem and the judgment of the world. The word " immediately " (Matt. xxiv. 29), is not to be taken as an indication of time. Jesus expressly says " of that day knoweth no man, not even the angels, neither the Son, but the Father " (Mark xiii. 32). It is to be interpreted as part of the language of apocalypse, and in accordance with the peculiar character of the prophetic vision. The triumph of righteousness, as manifested in any local judgment, is a prophecy and assurance of its final triumph, when the last great day of God's Assize has come. In the apocalyptic discourses of Jesus, the Parousia or Coming of the Son of Man is the apocalyptic symbol of His triumph. Everyone that opposed His will is to be judged and condemned, and those who assisted Him or suffered for His sake are to be accepted and rewarded.

3. It is most unfortunate that the Parousia of Christ has been generally interpreted as His Second Coming. That is a phrase which does not occur in the New Testament, and it is to some extent misleading. It does not give room for the idea that there may be many such Comings—an idea which is involved in the apocalyptic distinction between the " age " that now is and the " age " that is to come, an idea which is also forced upon us by the facts of history, and is justified by our Lord's interpretation of the destruction of the Jewish state as a coming of the Son of Man. The judgment which took place in Judæa may be repeated again and again in different centuries and countries.

The First Things of Jesus

It was the condemnation of a nation's life, the ending of an " age," the triumph of righteousness, or of Christ. Looked at in this way every nation has its " Day." The fall of empires, the decay of institutions, the passing away of forms or social organisations which are hoary with age and crime, are part of the history of the world, and might be described in the language of apocalypse, if it were in use at the present time. The great law of righteousness which rules among the inhabitants of the earth, even though they may be ignorant of it, produces the crises, brings in the judgment days in which nations change or pass. The wrongs which have become intolerable, the institutions of the state which through their corruption burden the lives of men, are at last openly condemned, opposed, or attacked. Their end usually comes through rebellion, revolution, or war, that " vast corrector of enormous crimes." There are tremendous upheavals, social cataclysms, the death-throes of an ancient order of things, and the birth-pangs of new conditions. To the eye of a seer, each of the great catastrophes of history would be a coming of the Day of the Lord, or a Parousia of the Lord Jesus, and they would all be linked with the " Day " when the world as a whole reaches the crisis of its course. As Schiller said, " The history of the world is the judgment of the world." Carlyle's

The Gospel must first be Preached

" French Revolution " is the nearest approach to an apocalypse which we have in modern literature. In his own peculiar style he emphasises the certain downfall of " shams " and tyrannies, and sets forth some of the invisible forces which work for righteousness or retribution in human history.

4. If we interpret the apocalyptic sayings of Jesus as apocalypses, we may see in His forecast of what was to happen to Jerusalem, an indication of what may take place again and again in the history of nations. He will come often, to end an age of a nation's life, and to bring in the triumph of righteousness. His forecast of the final judgment is a revelation of what is to happen, when all these sectional crises are summed up and ended at the close of the history of the world.

5. We are now in a position to understand the place which the preaching of the Gospel is to have in the future course of the world. We can answer the question, " Why, before the end, must the Gospel first be preached among all nations ? " The evangelist, Matthew, says it is for a witness (Matt. xxiv. 14). But a witness of what ? We need to realise what the preaching of the Gospel meant to Jesus. Until His coming, it was the law of righteousness written on the hearts of men, or proclaimed by prophets and teachers, by which men and nations were tried. Decay and destruction were the

Nemesis which followed disobedience. Slowly, but inevitably, the judgments of God fulfilled themselves. The nations which would not serve Him perished. The known or unknown principles of righteousness wrought out His will in national change or fall. But with the coming of Christ the world entered upon a new era of its history. The will of God was incarnated in a life ; His love as well as His righteousness was revealed. The record of them is in the Gospel. This new revelation of love and righteousness is now to work as a witness for God in the lives of men and nations. By it the institutions, conduct and forms of social organisation are to be tried and tested. The preaching of the Gospel brings to the knowledge of men the highest revelation of the holy will of God. It is the new force working in history, and leading men and nations to crisis and judgment.

It is thus that Jesus represents the effect of His words. He came not to send peace, but a sword. His truth is like leaven working with irresistible power. It sets men at variance one with another, even in the closest and tenderest relations of life —the son against the father, and the daughter against the mother. These forces of variance and division extend their influence gradually to national and social life. Slowly, but surely, the conflict becomes open and visible. The truth and spirit

The Gospel must first be Preached

of the Gospel touch the national life in its customs, and institutions, in its social and political forms of organisation. The guardians of the threatened interests set about defending them. Usually all the forces of a nation's might are in their hands. There is persecution, conflict, or disturbance. Wars and rumours of wars, social unrest, widespread suffering through the disorganisation of industry, and the disruption of the social order, are the results of the strife. Gradually the struggle reaches its crisis, and victory inclines to the one side or the other. Not always in the history of the world has the outcome of the conflict been the clear triumph of the Gospel. Other peoples besides the Jews have not known the time of their visitation. They have rejected the word of life and have gone on their darkened way to decay or death. But the decay of nations through the rejection of the Gospel, and their renascence through the acceptance of it, are alike the tokens of the Parousia of Christ.

It was so in the history of the Jewish state. The preaching of the Gospel was the influence which precipitated the crisis that led to its fall. Though the period of the personal ministry of Jesus was brief, yet, through the comparative smallness of the country, the commanding power of the personality of Jesus, combined with the work of His disciples, brought the knowledge of the

Gospel to the whole nation. It detached a large section of the people from the parties which sought the fulfilment of the patriotic dreams of an independent Jewish commonwealth. It brought to the rulers the possibility of a national religion and life which would be characterised by spirit and truth. The nation would have lived, though its institutions would have been changed, had they accepted the Gospel. But, having rejected the spiritual aims of the Lord Jesus, they were the more fanatically attached to the ideas which He opposed, and to the institutions which He condemned. Since they would not take His way, there was nothing left for them but to seek to carry out their own ambitions to their final issue. The conflict with the Romans was in reality a consequence of their refusal to submit to the guidance of Jesus in the preaching of the Gospel. The destruction of Jerusalem and the fall of the Jewish state were the judgment of God on national blindness and unrighteousness. The nation which would not serve Him in the fullest revelation of His holy will must perish. Reading that event apocalyptically, it was a Parousia of Christ.

The fall of the Roman empire was another such crisis in the history of the world. The preaching of the Gospel again precipitated the catastrophe. Into the vast unity of the empire of Rome the

The Gospel must first be Preached

leaven of Christianity was introduced. It wrought silently and invisibly for a time, but soon its effects became discernible. The Christians were regarded as the enemies of the state. The fierce energies of persecution were repeatedly employed to repress them, but the spirit of the new life escaped from the grasp of the physical might which sought to crush it, and spread the more widely through its escape. The whole strength of the empire spent itself in vain in the endeavour to destroy it. One institution after another succumbed to its influence. The temples were deserted or consecrated as churches. Jupiter, Venus, Minerva and all the host of subsidiary deities were swept away into the realm of mythology. Then also the free spirit of the Gospel quickened into activity the latent nationalism, which stirred within the wide circumference of the empire of Rome, and ultimately broke it into fragments. The division of the empire by Diocletian was a vain expedient to prevent the inevitable disruption. The invasion of the Goths was the touch from the outside, at which the grandeur of the world's mightiest empire fell. In apocalyptic language it was a day of the Lord, a Parousia of Christ. The classical type of life and rule and worship passed away in a cataclysm which shook the world. A new dispensation began its course. Christ and not Cæsar became the ruler of men, and the chief figure to whom their thoughts were turned.

At the time of the Reformation we see the same phenomena. The Church which had made itself heir to the rule of imperial Rome had grown corrupt, and the " Day " came when it must be tried by the truth it had betrayed. The power which brought on the crisis was the preaching of the Gospel by Luther and his followers. The leaven of its free and gracious spirit fermented in the minds of the people, till they were ready to revolt against the domination of the Pope. Again there were persecutions, conflicts, bitter wars, and vast-spread distress, but the doctrines of grace triumphed, the might of the Papacy was weakened, and the nations which hailed Christ as their only Head leaped to the forefront of the world's life. The seer would again describe it as a Parousia of the Son of Man.

In the French Revolution we see not so much the coming of the Son of Man, as a coming of the sons of men. It was the ideas of philosophers, rather than the preaching of the word, which led to that great crisis, and determined its results. The persecutions, massacres, and banishment of the Huguenots deprived France of the guidance of the Gospel in the day of her calamity. It was the fierce spirit of an atheistic passion, which revolted against

The Gospel must first be Preached

the tyrannies of the *ancien régime*, and sought the Rights of Man through a sea of blood. What the course and outcome of that dread upheaval might have been, had the spirit of the Gospel been the moving influence, none can tell, but assuredly they would have been widely different from what they actually were.

In India and China at the present day, we can recognise the beginning of what will ultimately lead to crises and changes, such as have followed the preaching of the Gospel elsewhere. The power of the new ideas, the influence of the Christian spirit, have already shown themselves. The Boxer persecutions were but a repetition of the policy of pagan Rome. Similar repressive attempts would have happened in India had it not been for the restraint of the governing power. But no one can listen to a missionary without learning that social persecution is widespread and grievous. The unrest of India has a double source—the instinct of liberty, quickened by the influence of Christianity through contact with Western civilisation, and the dread that the national institutions of social and religious life may be endangered. Stormy times are ahead in both of these Eastern lands. Their life and customs are being touched and tried by the truth of the Gospel. Change and upheaval are certain, till He comes whose right it is to reign.

The First Things of Jesus

When, and how, the final crisis of the world is to come no one knows, but its day is appointed. One thing only is certain that the Gospel must first be preached among all nations.

First Count the Cost

"In the long run we really love the sternest
things in life the best."—JOHN A. SYMONDS.

" Yet know, nor of the terms complain,
    Where Jesus comes He comes to reign ;
To reign, and with no partial sway,
    Thoughts must be slain that disobey.

JOSEPH GRIGG.

" If Thou, my Christ, to-day
  Shouldst come to me and say,
  What battles hast thou fought for Me ?
  Show Me thy scars, I fain would see
    Love's depth of victory.

" If Thou shouldst speak, my Christ,
  My Leader and my King,
  And bid me lay my wounds in sight,
    What love-scars would I bring ? "

CHAPTER V

"FIRST COUNT THE COST"

THE SUPREMACY OF OBEDIENCE TO CHRIST

The related parables of the wise builder and the
cautious king (Luke xiv. 28-32), were spoken at the
time when the popularity of Jesus was at its height.
They express with unmistakable emphasis His
desire that men should see, in the calm, clear light
of reason, all that was involved in discipleship.
He would have them take forethought like a man
who intended to build a tower. Such a work
demanded time and money, planning and perse-
verance. No one but a fool would begin it without
counting the cost. If he did, the result would
most likely be a " folly " which would stand as
a cause of scoffing to the whole countryside.

Even more impressively is the same lesson taught
in the careful forethought with which a king makes
war. The penalties of defeat are so great and
lasting, that none but the foolish engages in it
" with a light heart." Onerous conditions of peace
may be easier than the outcome of the dread arbitra-

ment of war. Jesus anticipates Moltke's motto, "Erst Wägen, dann Wagen." He would have men sit down first and count the cost of discipleship, realise the conflict which it involved, and then determine what they were to do.

1. But the cost and conflict arise in relation to forces and feelings which touch the lives of men most powerfully. The parables are prefaced by the words, " If any man come to Me, and hate not his father and mother, and children, and brothers and sisters, yea, and his own life also, he cannot be My disciple ; and whosoever doth not bear his cross and come after Me cannot be My disciple," and they are followed by the declaration, " So whosoever he be of you that forsaketh not all that he hath, he cannot be My disciple " (Luke xiv. 26, 27, 38). The claims of family relationships, the love of life, the dread of pain, the entanglements of worldly possessions, are the elements of cost and the forces of conflict in the lives of those who would follow Jesus. Over against these strong and subtle influences Jesus sets Himself as the supreme Lord of life. Obedience to Him is the first and last law of discipleship. His claim is primary ; all else is secondary. For His disciples the whole perspective of duty is revolutionised. One question alone is their absolute and final rule—" Lord, what wilt Thou have me to do ? " Eagerly as He longed

for disciples, He would have them on no lower terms. He conceals nothing of the cost, hides nothing of the conflict.

2. We cannot give too much importance to this declaration of the conditions of discipleship on the part of Jesus. He is really laying down a new basis of morality, introducing a principle which was subversive of the foundations on which the moral order of the time was built. Speaking generally, up till that time the State and the Family had been the chief factors and forces of moral life. It was only in connection with them that the individual had any rights or duties in relation to others, or even to God. The individual was bound to obey the claims of the national, tribal, or family organism to which he belonged. In process of time and thought, the conceptions of duty which were based on these relationships had lost much of their authority. The influence of prophetic teaching, the loss of national liberty, the effects of the Dispersion had weakened the claim of the State. The family was still the social unit, but its authority also had been lessened by the disorganisation of national life, and the claims of the Scribes and Pharisees on behalf of the Temple treasury (Matt. xv. 4-6). The old order was breaking up, and no other spiritual bond or sanction had been discovered. It was in these conditions that Jesus

introduced this new and revolutionary principle of moral life. Neither the State nor the Family, nor any other subordinate influence, was worthy of the place it held, or sufficient for the moral needs of men. Jesus now dethroned them, and set Himself in their stead, claiming the authority which they had exercised. Obedience to Him now became the supreme duty.

It is necessary to emphasise the significance of the declaration of Jesus in relation to the pre-existing moral order, if we are to understand the peculiarly striking terms in which it is expressed. The power of the ancient rulers of life had to be broken, before the new could be accepted. The revolutionary principle had to be stated in a form which was paradoxical in its emphasis, that it might make a due impression on the minds of men. The powers and influences which men had obeyed were still mighty; even yet they often claim supreme authority. In order that the new authority should be recognised, it had to be proclaimed in the most absolute terms. " If any man come to Me, and hate not his father and mother, and children and brothers and sisters, yea, and his own life also, he cannot be My disciple ; and whosoever doth not bear his cross and come after Me cannot be My disciple ; and whosoever he be of you that forsaketh not all that he hath, he cannot be My disciple." Jesus puts devotion to Himself above all else. We must not suppose that all the possibilities of conflict and sacrifice which are mentioned here, are to be experienced by every one who becomes a disciple of Jesus. The influences which most largely affect the lives of men are massed together, but each life may not be affected by them all. The determining factor of one life may have little power in the life of another. Family affection may be the chief consideration in one, the fear of death in another, the shrinking from pain in a third, and the love of money in a fourth. The list is not exhaustive. The principal moral forces are indicated, that all may be regarded as powers over which the Lord Jesus claims precedence. The influence to which any one is most subject, provides the test of the reality of devotion to Jesus. He comes to men in their different conditions of moral susceptibility, and claims the right to be the ruler of their lives. The authority which predominates in any individual life must yield to that of Jesus. Separate incidents might be found in the Gospels which illustrate the conflict of the claim of Jesus with each of these different influences mentioned here. The whole of the Gospel history may be regarded as the revelation and assertion of the claim of Jesus to be the ruler of the conscience of mankind.

The First Things of Jesus

In making Himself the centre of the new moral order, Jesus established a universal rule over the souls of men, apart from their relation to any existing form of associated life. He gave them a law which would suffice, even if they were to live singly and alone. By uniting men to Himself, He emancipated them from the overwhelming influences of social and national relationships, gave them personal rights and duties, made the individual of infinite worth to himself, because he was of infinite worth to Him. It is not too much to say that the conscience of man was liberated from the bondage in which it had been held, when Jesus declared that He was its Lord.

3. The moral authority which Jesus claims is not only new, but it is tacitly assumed to be better than the old. No other reason could justify such a revolutionary proposal in regard to the supreme standard of duty. The will of Christ must present a nobler ideal of life, provide stronger inspirations to obedience, supply weightier sanctions for its behests, afford greater sufficiency to meet the varied conditions in which men find themselves in need of guidance, and secure grander results in conduct and character than all the old ruling conceptions and influences put together. The conflict in which the follower of Jesus has to engage arises not only from the strife between the old

and the new, but from the opposition between lower and higher forms of moral authority. Whatever keeps men from obeying the highest law, or fulfilling the noblest duty, can rightly be regarded as hateful. The good that is possible is left undone, the finest qualities of the soul remain unexercised, the heights of moral achievement which are within its reach are unattained. When the good is the enemy of the best, the good may be rightly hated.

This is readily admitted when it is the love of one's own life which is the hindrance. The strength of the instinct of self-preservation is universally recognised. Perhaps there is no more generally potent influence working in the hearts of men. Its power is expressed in the words of Satan, " All that a man hath will he give for his life " (Job ii. 4). The sneer is a slander on humanity, and is not true universally. But the instinct has wrought most hurtfully wherever it has become dominant. Through mere love of life, or dread of death, men have shunned the way of duty and turned aside from the call of heroic endeavour. The instinct has its uses, for it is divinely implanted, but the sphere of its action should be carefully limited. It must not intrude into matters of moral necessity. It is a commonplace even of pagan morality that to noble-minded men a thousand things are to be preferred to mere existence. Life may be preserved at the cost of all that makes life worth living. We approve of the saying of Pompey who, when warned on one occasion of the dangers which would meet him if he ventured to go to Rome, replied, " It is not necessary that I should live, but it is necessary that I should go to Rome." We also recognise that Dr. Johnson gave the final answer to the plea, " One must live," which was once spoken in his hearing, when he said, " I don't see the necessity ! " The claims of the moral life of man must ever be held as higher than those of the physical. The cowardly thoughts which course through the minds of men, urging them to shrink from duties which involve danger or death, spring from the lower instincts of human nature, and are hostile to the higher. They ought not to stand for a moment as barriers in the way of doing what conscience declares to be right. The true man will hate them as he feels their power, will show his manhood by casting them from him, and treading them under foot as things abhorred. It is in this sense that we are to understand the demand that men should hate their own lives, if they would follow Christ. The noble army of martyrs, who overcame the sharpness of death in the arena or the prison, gained the crown of life, because they counted not their lives dear unto themselves, that they might be faithful to their Lord and Saviour.

First Count the Cost

They hated their own life that they might do His will.

This also is the sense in which we are to understand the demand for hatred of father and mother, and brothers and sisters. These family relationships are the source of many of the loveliest things in human life. Motherhood in the height of its sacrifice ; fatherhood in its tender strength, childhood in the beauty of its reverence and dependence, and all the happy intimacies of the home—these simple pieties make the family a school of the noblest life and a glory of the world. Its authority is very great, for it speaks in the tones of affection ; obedience is instinctive and generally unquestioned, for it seeks the good of those whom it controls. Jesus seems to be striking at the most sacred and rightful human authority, when He bids His followers hate those to whom they are bound by the kindliest of earthly ties. But He saw that the authority of the family relationships did not cover the whole of moral life. It was not enough to be a good parent, a dutiful child, a loving brother or sister. The morality of the home was not always right in its instructions ; its restraints were often hurtful and unwise, it sometimes missed and even opposed the highest good. Selfish love might hinder the soul in its obedience to duty and endeavour after right. Jesus claimed to be a wiser, higher, better guide. He dared to put Himself in the place which the family had held in the lives of those who called Him Lord. He Himself had to resist the influence of His mother, and the interference of His brethren. In their loving ignorance they would have kept Him from doing His Father's will. They were stumbling-blocks in His way which He resolutely set aside. He saw that this painful experience of His must be repeated in all who followed Him. The higher vision of duty which He revealed would often conflict with the lower conceptions of right in the minds of their relatives. As followers of the best, they must hate all who would keep them from it ; hate them because they loved them, and loved them the more dearly because they loved Christ. The struggle which Millais represented in the picture of the Huguenot lovers is the struggle to which Christ calls all who follow Him. They must say—

> " I could not love thee, dear, so much,
> Loved I not honour more."

In the happy atmosphere of family affection, the soul may live on, never dreaming that the obedience which is due to the family authority may become questionable, or that new light may be thrown upon the way of duty. But when the awakening comes, and the call of Christ is heard, it brings not peace but a sword, setting a man at variance with those who are nearest and dearest to him. Can we imagine anything more terrible than an experience like that, especially in the early days, when the claim of Christ as Lord of the soul was not recognised as it is to-day ? It was where devotion to Christ was deepest, and family affection strongest, that the most bitter conflict would take place. The more clearly the follower of Christ saw the way which He pointed out, the more must he hate the ignorant affection which would hinder him from treading it.

There is no difficulty in relation to the saying, " Whosoever doth not bear his cross and come after Me, cannot be My disciple." It is a heroic life to which Jesus calls mankind ; it involves hardship, sacrifice and pain. But it is strange that even before He bore His cross, the cross should be to Him the great symbol of pain and uttermost self-sacrifice. One wonders if it was He who first gave it this significance, and if He did so because, even then, the Cross of Calvary had cast its shadow over His life, and He saw that all self-sacrifice which was involved in following Him was identical with His own. It is as if He said, " It is enough for the disciple that he be as his Master." To follow Him was to share in His spirit, and therefore also to share in His suffering. There is no escape from the cross, even if escape were desired. Discipleship is impossible without it. The endurance of manhood and the patience of womanhood find their exercise in His service. However strange it may seem to us, we know that every step upward is won by pain. " Perfected by suffering " is the illuminating word. They who would be like Christ must pass through the same discipline. We give up the dream of gaining the crown when we shrink from the cross ; we miss the blessing when we shun the burden. If we would reign with Christ we must suffer with Him, and obedience to His call involves it.

But what shall we say of the demand, " Whosoever he be of you who forsaketh not all that he hath, cannot be My disciple ? " It is not to be read as a universal requirement of poverty on the part of the disciples of Jesus. It is like the other demands, an illustration of the claim of Jesus to absolute control. It may best be understood from what was said to the rich young ruler who came to Him with the cry, " What shall I do that I may inherit eternal life ? " Jesus looking on him loved him, and said, " Sell what thou hast and give to the poor, and come, follow Me." But he went away sorrowful, for he had great possessions. We must not think that Jesus had no place in His company for rich men, though it is a very strait gate by which they enter, nor are we to understand that this one had a miser's spirit. How could Jesus have loved him had it been so ?   He was one who said that he had kept the law from his youth.   But his life was really dominated by his wealth.   He owed his place in society to it, his chiefest interests were associated with it.   If he would serve Christ he must lay his wealth at His feet.   The demand that he should sell his possessions was simply the *personal* test of his readiness to give the guidance of his life into the keeping of Christ.   It was an assertion of the claim which was involved in the command, " Come, follow Me."   The love of wealth, not necessarily for its own sake, but for the freedom and power which it gave him,was the influence that ruled his soul, and Jesus asked that He should be accepted as the ruler instead.   It is eventually the same request as He made in all other cases.   The sensitive spirit that shrinks from pain, and orders life so as to avoid it, must yield up its sheltered security ; the timid soul, subject to bondage through the fear of death, must sacrifice its precautions ; the son, submissive to the rule of parents, must be ready to cast aside his greatest reverence : all must yield complete obedience to the will of Jesus.

5. But the new and higher authority does not simply displace the old.   It embraces within it all the duties which the old sought to enforce, and reproduces them in a nobler and loftier form.   The claims of family relationship are never so fully

recognised, or so beautifully fulfilled, as when Christ is their motive. The Christian home is the ideal home of the world, and it surpasses all earlier or other conceptions in its helpfulness, its charm and its peace. The dread of pain has been transformed into the dread of giving pain. The soul that was sensitive for itself has been made sensitive for others ; the susceptibility that made it shrink from what would hurt, has been recreated in the spirit of compassion—a spirit finely touched to a fine issue. Wealth is never rightly gained or rightly used until Christ becomes its sovereign. The use of wealth is the secret for which the world is waiting, but it may be learned at the feet of Christ. The problems of poverty, the embarrassments of the millionaire, await the day when the guidance of Jesus is loyally accepted. As for the fear of death, Jesus has dispelled it altogether from the outlook of His followers. He has " abolished " it; " brought life and immortality to light by the Gospel," and " opened the kingdom of heaven to all believers."

Christ as the Lord of the soul has justified His claims. The results of His rule, wherever it has been accepted in spirit and in truth, have transformed the world. The Christian centuries are His witnesses. But what shall we say of Him who, as a humble teacher from a highland village of the subject land of Palestine, set Himself in the place of all the powers that ruled the lives of men ? Who is this who dares to overthrow all the authorities and sanctities which men had reverenced and obeyed ; who demands that His will shall be done, it matters not who opposes or what may be the cost of obedience, and, greatest wonder of all, has received the homage which He claimed throughout the Christian centuries ? Shall we say that He is simply a man, like the rest of us, with only a little more of the Spirit of God in His heart ?

The teachers of the ages say, " Seek the right, follow the truth, be faithful to the best and highest that you know or that I can teach you." Jesus is alone in saying, " Follow Me." He puts Himself in the place which is His by right. We give the reason why when we say

> " Thou art the King of Glory, O Christ !
> Thou art the everlasting Son of the Father ! "

First Preach the Gospel

"Preach the Word; be instant in season, out of season."—ST. PAUL.

"Whatever hazards you run, go on with your work, publishing and proclaiming the everlasting Gospel to all the world; that is your business, mind that."—MATTHEW HENRY.

"Give me one hundred men who hate nothing but sin, fear nothing but God, and are 'determined to know nothing but Jesus Christ and Him crucified,' and I will turn the world upside down."

JOHN WESLEY.

"Professor Elmslie, in the brief delirium before death, when his mind was wandering, came back over and over again to 'God is Love; I will go out and tell this to all the world; they do not know it.'"

CHAPTER VI

"FIRST PREACH THE GOSPEL"

IF we compare the parallel passages, Matt. viii. 18-23 and Luke ix. 57-62, we make the interesting discovery that two of the three men who appear in the incidents recorded by St. Luke were already disciples of Jesus—using that term in its broad and general sense. The likelihood is that the third man stood in the same relation to Jesus. This is a point of great importance, for it provides the key to the right interpretation of the incidents. What was before the three men at the moment was the possibility of becoming members of the little company of companion-disciples, who were being trained for the work of Apostleship.

The three incidents may not have happened at the same time, but they are grouped together because they illustrate one great principle. They indicate the place which the Lord Jesus assigned to the duty of preaching the Gospel. They express His sense of its urgency. They inculcate most impressive lessons for every preacher, and have an abiding significance for the Church of Christ in every age and land.

It must be remembered that, at the time when these incidents took place, the work for which Jesus was calling and training His disciples was new. The wise men of Greece never thought of spreading the light of Hellenism throughout the world. They did not believe that the Barbarians were capable of receiving it. The rhetoricians of Rome had nothing to speak of that was of universal worth or interest. It was the beneficence of Law and Order which was Rome's peculiar gift to the world, and that was spread abroad by the might of the armed legions, not by a preached word. The Jews of the Greek Dispersion maintained an active proselytising propaganda, but Judaism as a whole discouraged it, and looked upon the proselytes as a " plague of leprosy." Although the Jews believed themselves to have exclusive possession of " the oracles of God," they did not realise that it was their duty or privilege to publish the truth to other nations. The " middle wall of partition " built by racial and religious distinctions, and strengthened by centuries of mutual contempt, effectively shut out the Gentile world as a possible sphere of labour for Jewish teachers. The chief concern of the orthodox Jew was to keep separate from the Gentile. In Palestine organised evangelisation such as Jesus contemplated was unknown. The Law had been developed into such an elaborate and intricate system of rules and regulations that knowledge of it was confined to a professional class, and any popular presentation of its contents was impossible. When Jesus said " To the poor the Gospel is preached," He introduced an original practice. When He called men that they might be trained for this work, He was preparing them for work which was entirely new. As such its importance had to be emphasised; its urgency had to be made clear. The conditions of service had to be realised, and Jesus seized the opportunity which was offered in the circumstances of the three men, to impress these things on the minds of His disciples.

It is the imperative importance of the claims of the Gospel on those who are to preach it which is set forth in these incidents, and in such an unforgettable way.

1. The Scribe was the first candidate for Apostleship. In the Gospel according to St. Matthew, his offer of service was made shortly after Jesus had delivered the Sermon on the Mount. But, prior to the Sermon, Jesus had chosen from the general company of disciples the men who were to be with Him in His itinerant ministry. This Scribe may have cherished secret longings that he might be one of them. But Jesus had not called

him. The Master, with the chosen Twelve, went down to the shore to take ship for the other side of the lake. It was then that the Scribe made this effort to obtain his heart's desire. " Master," he cried, " I will follow Thee whithersoever Thou goest." But Jesus refused, saying, " The foxes have holes, and the birds of the air have nests, but the Son of Man hath not where to lay His head." Why did Jesus answer thus ? Volunteers were rare in His experience, why did He refuse one when he came forward ? We cannot think it was because the Scribe had " earthly aims which the eye of Jesus fully penetrated."* That reason would have excluded the men who said, " Behold, we have forsaken all and followed Thee ; what shall we have therefore ? " (Matt. xix. 27). Neither is it likely that he was rejected because he was of a rash and impulsive temperament, or how could St. Peter have been one of the Twelve ? What then was the reason ?

The Master's words have a reference to certain physical privations which He and His followers had to endure. The itinerant character of His public ministry involved an almost continual uncertainty of obtaining shelter. In one instance we know that hospitality was refused, and that may have occurred more frequently. Even though the

* Godet. " Commentary on St. Luke's Gospel," *in loco*.

country was thickly populated, and hospitality was a general virtue, it might happen that the necessities of the itineracy, and the comparative largeness of the company, would compel Jesus and His followers to pass the night in the open air. These are the possibilities which are involved in the graphic words in which the offer of the Scribe is refused, but they provide a clue which we may follow. There was some physical disability in this eager volunteer. He was a scribe, and most likely had all the bodily characteristics associated with his profession. He was unaccustomed to hardship ; his sedentary occupation unfitted him for an out-door life, which involved exposure to a greater or less degree. " The spirit was willing, but the flesh was weak." But more than willingness was required. The work of preaching the Gospel, especially at that early time, was too important to be entrusted to one who might not be physically fit for the task. The message of the love and grace of God must not be endangered or hindered through the breakdown of the messenger. No general would choose, as the bearer of an important despatch, one who might not be able to bear the toil and exposure of the journey. So he who would engage in the " King's business " must be equal to the strain which it involves. No amount of eagerness or personal desire would serve if it was likely that the volunteer would fail or fall under the inevitable hardships of an itinerant ministry. The success of the work was of more importance than the feelings of the man who wanted to engage in it.

This Scribe may be taken as the type of many men and women who have to bear the cross of physical weakness, and all its consequence limitations, whose spirit and devotion would send them forth to work for Christ in the high places of the field. Every missionary committee has experienced the sadness of saying, gently but resolutely, that while the spiritual qualifications in some volunteer for the foreign field are all that can be desired, the physical constitution is not fit for the strain. It may have been because of this necessity of physical fitness, that so many of the Twelve were hardy fishermen, men tanned by the sun and the sea, inured to hardship, and accustomed to exposure. Like the angels of God, these messengers of the Cross must " excel in strength." Did not Richter say, " In this world we must not only have wings for the empyrean, but a stout pair of boots for the paving-stones " ?

We believe it was on account of physical unfitness that the Scribe was rejected, but that he was rejected lovingly. Surely, Jesus, looking on him, loved him, and sent him away with great peace in his heart! He could serve Him still, though not in the way of his desire. He learned the lesson which we also need to learn, that the wish to serve Christ in the preaching of the Gospel is not enough. At all costs of personal feeling the work must succeed. The interests of the Gospel are supreme.

These thoughts apply most aptly to mission work in the foreign field, but they have a keen and painful edge for preachers at home. Whatever happens to the preacher whose health has broken down, he must not allow any interest or feeling of his own to stand in the way of the progress of the Gospel. The servants of Christ must be of the Master's mind, that the interests of the work are the first consideration. Like the great Apostle they must be ready to "suffer all things," lest they should hinder the Gospel of Christ. To cling to the office of the preacher, when one is no longer fit for the duty which belongs to it, is to expose oneself to the severest sentence from the lips of Christ. Workers who break down may be certain of His sympathy and care, as they should be of the sympathy and care of all amongst whom they have broken the Bread of Life, but no interest or feeling of theirs is to stand for a moment in the way of the Gospel. That is the matter which was definitely and finally settled here.

2. The second man was called by Jesus. It was a call like that which had been given to Peter and John—a call to enter the band of companion-

disciples who were to be trained for Apostleship. But he did not understand the importance or urgency of the call. Another duty bulked more largely in his mind. He said, " Suffer me first to go and bury my father." In the East the duty here referred to is of much greater importance than it is amongst ourselves. In India, where many of the customs of the Bible are to be seen at work, it is regarded as the greatest of calamities, if a man has not a son to pay to his body the last reverences of affection. The son will not go far from home if his father has been seized with illness, or is evidently near to death. In the present case the father was not dead. If his body had actually been awaiting burial the son would have been unclean, and could not have mingled with the crowd. Most likely the father was an old man ; death had not come, but it was not far away. In these circumstances, the son felt that he could not engage in a mission which would take him away from home. It may be that he was unwilling, and covered his shrinking with this seemly excuse. But how would Jesus who " knew what was in man " have called him if that had been the case ? We incline to believe that he was willing to go, but that the thought of his duty to his father prevented him. The call of Jesus is of itself a testimony to the worth of the man.

First Preach the Gospel

It was a sense of filial duty which led him to ask for delay but Jesus said, " Let the dead bury their own dead, but go thou and preach the Kingdom of God." Again we ask, why did Jesus who cared so tenderly for His mother, and gave to family affection its strongest sanctions, reply to this man in this way ? Our answer is the same as before. Men who are to serve in the Gospel must learn that there is no other duty which is of equal or higher importance. This man was already a disciple, one of the few at that time who were alive from the dead. He was fitted to be a preacher of the word of life. There were countless numbers who could attend to the duties of burial ; he must give himself, without reserve, to the more imperative duty of saving souls. No surgeon on the field of battle, with thousands of wounded lying around him, would allow one of his skilled assistants to help in burying the dead.* That is a needful work but there are others who can attend to it. He who is qualified to save life must devote himself to the higher duty which the others cannot do. It is thus that the Lord Jesus regards the work of the preachers of the Gospel. He would give to His disciples His own profound conviction of the infinite worth and absolute need of the truth He was proclaiming. The world was dying from the wounds

* Dykes, "Expositor." Third Series, vol. ii, p. 292.

of sin, and he who could carry the healing grace of the Gospel must not spend time and energy on things of lesser moment, however right and seemly they might be.

The summons of war has such urgency that no one dares to hesitate. Scorn and hissing would be the portion of any sworn servant of the king, who asked that he might wait at home till he buried his father, while the old man was yet alive. Even the request for leave to go home to say good-bye, might be thought unreasonable or at least as untimely. Sir Walter Scott tells how, as the Fiery Cross passed through the Western Highlands

> " The fisherman forsook the strand ;
> The swarthy smith took dirk in hand ;
>
> .   .   .   .
>
> The herds without a keeper strayed ;
> The plough was in the furrow stayed ;
> The falc'ner toss'd his hawk away ;
> The hunter left the hawk at bay ;
> Prompt at the signal of alarms,
> Each son of Alpine rush'd to arms."

If the call of war is so urgent that everything else must stand aside, is it not right that the call to the service of the Gospel of Peace should have at least an equally imperative note ?

The urgency of the Gospel is a truth which requires to be remembered by the Church and by her preachers in all ages, but never more than at the

First Preach the Gospel

present time. The numerous organisations which have been called into activity in connection with the Christian Church, have thrown upon preachers a vast burden of duties, which make large claims on their time and strength. As things are at present, many a preacher, hearing afresh the note of urgency in the command to preach, has to cry " God be merciful to me, a sinner ! " The danger is one that showed itself in the earliest days of the Church's life. In view of it St. Peter said, " It is not reason that we should leave the word of God and serve tables." Even though it is recognised that preachers at home are not like missionaries among the heathen, can we for a moment think that the needs of our land are so slight, that it is not necessary to insist any longer on the urgency of the Gospel ? May it not be that those who hear the Gospel from our lips to-day are encouraged to listen with respectful indifference, because they do not recognise the note of urgency in what we say ? The next revival, for which we hope and pray, may come when the Church of Christ hears again the stern and imperious word of the Master, and sets those who can preach the Gospel free from the service of tables, to give themselves entirely to the ministry of the Word. To set Christ before men is the essential duty of the Church which bears His name. All other forms of help will only " heal the hurt " of the world " slightly." None but Christ, and nothing but His salvation, can bring the healing which it needs. The same necessity lies upon preachers to-day as lay upon him who cried, " Woe is unto me if I preach not the Gospel ! " Ours is " the one talent it is death to hide."

3. It is the same lesson which is repeated in another form in the last of the three. He was a volunteer for Apostleship. It was not a confession of faith which he made when he said, " Lord, I will follow Thee." It was an offer of service. There is not a word too much in his expression of devotion. It is simple, direct, complete, but it is marred by the condition attached to it, " Let me first go bid them farewell which are at home at my house." His hesitation sprang from a loving regard to the feelings of those who were related to him. Elisha made the same request, when the call to take up the work of a prophet came to him from the lips of Elijah. Then it was granted, but now a new urgency in the mission of Jesus led to a refusal. The work of Jesus brooks no delay, and yields to no other interest. Therefore to him it is said, " No man, having put his hand to the plough, and looking back, is fit for the Kingdom of God." It is needless to suppose that Jesus saw a possible source of weakness in the affectionate nature of this man, and that He wished to protect him from the home influences

which might restrain him from carrying out his decision. The danger did not lie in any pleadings of foolish love which might await him at his house. It lay in himself, in the preference which he gave to the call of affection over the call of Christ, in the subordination of the work of preaching to the desire of pleasing his friends or himelf. He, too, had to learn once for all that this was not permitted. Most likely he was a husbandman, familiar with the work of the fields. He had often put his hands to the plough, and knew how needful it was to give undivided and unwavering attention to its guidance. Jesus answers him with an illustration which gained its power from his personal experience. As the plough must be guided with a single eye to the end of the furrow, so the Gospel must be preached with stedfast concentration. As the ploughman must allow nothing to distract his attention from the line which he is following, so the preacher must not suffer himself to be drawn aside from the work in which he is engaged. No other interest or object is to take up his thought or withdraw his mind from it.

Possibly our translation of the Saviour's words suggests a harsher interpretation than is warranted by them in the original. " Not fit for the Kingdom of God " is an awful sentence. It may be applied to cases which were not in the mind of Jesus when

He uttered it. He was not thinking of entrance into the Kingdom, but of service in it. His little parable is one of work. The words " not fit " should be translated " not well fit,"* that is, " not serviceable " or " not useful," in the work of the Kingdom of God. The ploughman who would draw a clean straight furrow must not look behind him. If he does so the furrow may be made, but it will be irregular, crooked, broken. Imagine a field ploughed in such a fashion ! No farmer would regard such a ploughman as serviceable in the field. He might still keep him on the farm, but the plough would be taken out of his hands.

What a lesson is here for all preachers ! They are only serviceable in the work of the Gospel who do it whole-heartedly. Each must say, " This one thing I do," else he will be an " unprofitable servant." Ah ! how many of those who are ploughing in the field of the world for the Son of Man may be rejected by Him ! How many are the interests which take away our thoughts from the work to which we have devoted ourselves ! These may be innocent, but they are distracting. They may be pleasant, but they are unprofitable. No severer judgment could be passed on a monarch than that which Gibbon pronounced on the Emperor Gallienus : " He was the master of several curious but useless

* εὐθετος.

sciences, a ready orator, an elegant poet, a skilful gardener, an excellent cook, and most contemptible prince."* But a similar judgment may await the *dilettante* preacher. Even in a Christian land he who serves Christ in the Gospel must have no side issues for his energies. Everything must be subordinated to the preaching of the Gospel. All other interests which attract him are only permissible if they become helpful in the supreme work of his life. " Happy is he who condemneth not himself in the thing which he alloweth."

4. But if there is such urgency and importance in the preaching of the Gospel, there must be an equal significance in the hearing of it, and a similar readiness and wholeheartedness in the acceptance of it. If there is " Woe " to the servant of Christ who does not preach the Gospel, much more is there " Woe " to those who hear and do not receive it. There is no duty or interest which ought to come before that. To be right with God ; to be taken out of the darkness of sin into the light of the love of God ; what else in the imperativeness of its need, or in the greatness of its blessing, is equal to that ? Neglect or delay is indicative of a blindness which prefers the " pleasures of sin " or " the fleeting vanities of this transitory world " to the abiding joy and peace and fulness of eternal life. " What

* "Decline and Fall of the Roman Empire," vol. i, chap. x.

shall it profit a man if he gain the whole world and lose his own soul ? " Until men see that, they know not the mind of Christ as to the worth of the soul, or the infinite loss which it suffers when He is neglected. To Him salvation is man's first interest. " To-day if ye will hear His voice, harden not your hearts." " We beseech you—in Christ's name, be ye reconciled to God."

Seek First the Kingdom of God

"Money is the God of our time, and Rothschild is his prophet."—HEINE.

"It is surely a proof of folly to devote ourselves wholly to that with which our supreme good has no connection."—THOMAS À KEMPIS.

"Man's chief end is not to be rich here, but to be rich toward God."—DENNEY.

"We sow the glebe and reap the corn,
And build the house where we may rest,
And then at moments suddenly
We look up to the great wide sky,
Inquiring wherefore we were born."
MRS. BROWNING.

"The highest morality may prove also to be the highest wisdom, when the half-told story comes to be finished."—CONAN DOYLE.

CHAPTER VII

"SEEK FIRST THE KINGDOM OF GOD"

THERE is no sentence which so distinctively expresses the mind of Jesus regarding the highest rule of life as " Seek ye first the Kingdom of God and His righteousness " (Matt. vi. 33). It gathers up everything into itself. It is His definition of the chief good which is within the reach of men. Many other words of His may be taken as ruling principles of life, but they are only parts of this simple and sublime utterance. It is the " secret of Jesus "; the clue which He put into the hands of men to guide them through the labyrinth of life.

1. At first sight it might seem that the words were spoken only to those who were burdened with anxiety as to what they should eat and drink, and wherewithal they should be clothed. But from a study of the preceding context it becomes evident that this regal and illuminating counsel is the conclusion of the section of the Sermon on the Mount, which is included within verses 19-33 of the sixth chapter. In that passgae reference is made to

two classes of men—to those who are seeking " treasure upon earth," and those who are absorbed in the effort to secure the things needful for the body. When the two classes are put together, they embrace the whole human family. Both are concerned about material things. Their energies and aspirations and anxieties go out in the same direction, and on the same lines, and the great rule is intended for both.

Many of the deep-reaching principles of Jesus were spoken in opposition to those of the Scribes and Pharisees, but in this instance He passes beyond the ideas of any sect or class, and sets forth His thought of the chief aim of life in contrast to what was universally held then, and is also widely, if not universally, held now. In His moral perspective the desirable things of life are arranged in a startlingly new order, and with a surprisingly strong emphasis. He places first what men degrade to a very subordinate position. In the foreground, as men's highest and best good, He sets the quest for the Kingdom of God.

2. It is easy to understand what men usually place in that position of honour and supreme desire. They are material things—" treasures upon earth," or " what we shall eat or drink, or wherewithal we shall be clothed." They may be described as the prizes of the world, or the necessities of the

natural life of man. In one form or another, these are thought to be the things of greatest importance and value. It is these which bulk most largely in the minds of men, and towards which their desires and ambitions are most strenuously directed. It is difficult for some to see why they should be set aside by the Lord Jesus, as unworthy to compete with the ideal which He sets up. The instinct of possession which lies behind all efforts after the " treasures upon earth," is deeply rooted in humanity and has an amazing strength. In spite of its excesses it cannot be said to be evil. The triumphs of civilisation, the treasures of art, the opportunities of science, and some of the greatest means of enriching and elevating the life of man, are the fruits of its energy. The progress of the world is intimately connected with the accumulation of material possessions. Even the best of men are limited in their efforts to benefit their fellows by the lack of such means as wealth provides.

Then there is also the instinct to preserve existence. It, too, is deeply rooted, intensely strong, and universal. We must eat and drink that we may live. The need is urgent and persistent. It is the driving force which animates the varied activities of the vast majority of humankind. Men plough the fields and reap the corn, dig in the mine and sail the sea, that they may find what they shall eat and drink and wherewithal they shall be clothed. The dark shadow of physical want is never far away from the mass of men. The dread of poverty, the fear of sickness, the uncertainty of employment, the relentless approach of age with all its disabilities, the thousand and one chances which threaten the means of livelihood, haunt the souls of the toiling millions and infest their minds with care. Nothing seems more right and reasonable than anxiety and effort to obtain food and clothing for ourselves and those who are dependent on us. We repeat with thorough approval the words of St. Paul, " If a man provide not for his own, and especially for those of his own household, he hath denied the faith, and is worse than an infidel."

3. Yet it is over against these useful and dutiful absorptions of men that Jesus sets His ideal of the quest of the Kingdom of God. There is no difficulty in knowing what He meant by that. Most of His parables are parables of the Kingdom ; the Sermon on the Mount is the Law of the Kingdom ; the Lord's Prayer is the prayer of the Kingdom—the whole of the Gospels is the Gospel of the Kingdom. It is that condition of life which arises in the soul and in the world, when the Heavenly Father is reverenced and trusted as the Sovereign Ruler of men ; when His loving and gracious will is done on earth as it is done in heaven. To seek the Kingdom

Seek First the Kingdom of God

of God is to live for the realisation of His holy will, to trust and serve and obey Him with the glad and loving spirit of a child. It means righteousness, truth, and purity—love and trust and tenderness. To do the things which please God becomes the supreme aim and joy of the soul.

An ideal like this seems strange and visionary as compared with the common aims of men. It appears unfit to compete for a moment with the stern and solid actualities of earthly existence. It has all the apparent unsubstantiality of a mystic dream. Yet with all earnestness Jesus distinctly sets it forth as the highest good that men can seek. The Kingdom of God is better than money, position or fame ; it is better also than food and clothing. The spiritual is higher than the material ; the things of the soul are of greater moment than the things of the body. The Kingdom of God is alone worthy of the first place in the thoughts and activities of men.

It is not difficult to see that the Kingdom of God is better than the wealth of the world. But to many our Lord seems unpractical, out of touch with reality, in setting the Kingdom of God above the things needful for the body. It is as if He, who had compassion on the multitudes and fed the hungry, were ignoring the needs and miseries of men ; as if He, who claimed to be the Truth, were talking nonsense, when He bids them give their first thought and effort to this unworldly business. The claims of the Kingdom may come in after the claims of the body have been satisfied, for how can men who are suffering from hunger and cold be convinced that there is any higher or more urgent duty than that of getting food and clothing ? So men argue, and yet Jesus judges men by their preferences in these matters. To Him it is the mark of a Gentile, that is, of a heathen, when the things needful for the body are the chief care. It is the sign of a child of God, when he seeks first the Kingdom of Heaven.

4. How are these conflicting cares to be reconciled ? How shall the opposing ideals of Christ and the world be harmonised ? To begin with, it is not thought for " these things " which is spoken of here, but " anxious thought," absorbing care, in which everything else is lost sight of. Then, the ideals of Christ and the world are not opposed as good and bad, or as right and wrong, but as first and second. It is a total misapprehension of our Lord's words to say that He forbids His followers to *think* of getting the wealth of the world, or of securing " what they shall eat or drink or wherewithal they shall be clothed." He is not careless of the power that is latent in material possessions, or indifferent to the natural and irrepressible needs

of men. He did not mean that they who called Him " Master " should impoverish themselves. Mary of Bethany was not rebuked for possessing " the box of ointment very precious." It is no part of His Gospel that only poor men can be His disciples. His invitation is addressed to all classes and conditions of men : " whosoever will " may come to Him. Nor did He give the least ground for the idea that His followers should make no effort to provide for the needs of the body. A disciple of Christ may be a man of wealth, or an eager and diligent worker to provide the necessities of physical existence. Such things have to do with the lives of men. They are of great importance, but not of first importance.   Their place is absolutely secondary.

Men's fault and folly lie in seeking them as if they were primary and essential ; in making them the treasures of the soul ; in thinking of them with anxious and absorbing care, as if they supplied the supreme need of life. The Kingdom of God is not set in opposition to the things of the world for which men seek ; *it is set above them.* It belongs to a realm that is higher than the physical and the material. It has to do with the essential life of man—a life that is more than existence, more than meat, more than riches. Man is a child of earth and time, but he is also a child of God—a spiritual being, made in His image, with power to think His thoughts and live in fellowship with Him. All thought and effort which are dominated by a lower conception of man's nature are misdirected. They leave him unsatisfied and undeveloped. The riddle of our life is never solved until we say, " Thou hast made us for Thyself and our hearts are restless until they rest in Thee."* We should call that man blind and foolish who starved himself that he might be clothed in fine raiment, but he also is blind and foolish who neglects the needs of the soul, that he may secure wealth or the means of existence. The moment that we realise the meaning of the Kingdom of God and the true character of the life of man, we see that it must be so. The Kingdom of God is righteousness and peace and joy in the Holy Ghost. It is living in union and communion with God as a child with a loving Father, delighting in His will, rejoicing in His love, finding our sweetest pleasure in what pleases Him.

When once the vision of that blessedness dawns upon the soul, there can be no question as to what is the highest and best good that men can seek. The Kingdom of God, which embraces all spiritual wealth and blessing, stands supreme. Righteousness is better than riches. The peace of God that passeth all understanding is sweeter far than all

* Augustine.

that can be gained without it. The joy of a spirit, which can be touched to fine issues by the impulse of the Spirit of God, is deeper and more lasting than all the joys that come from material possessions. In its saner moments the world itself agrees with Christ. It raises its monuments of praise to the good, and buries in its sepulchre of honour those who have lived for unselfish and unworldly ends, whose characters have won its homage by their lustre of purity and truth and love.

5. When the Kingdom of God is lifted to the place of supremacy, the ideals of the world find their proper sphere and usefulness. The treasures of the world may be sought by a follower of Jesus, provided only that the Kingdom of God is the highest rule and strongest passion of his life. It will guide him in seeking them, and in using them. They will become a means of serving God; a trust of which man is a steward. They will be sought not as an end in themselves, but as elements of usefulness and instruments of power, in the advancement of the Kingdom of God. All methods of gain will be controlled by the will of God, and whatever cannot stand the test of His righteousness and love will be refused and rejected.

So, too, when the Kingdom of God becomes the dominant principle of the soul, men may think of " what they shall eat or drink or wherewithal they may be clothed." The means of living will never be sought in ways that are alien to the will of God ; anxiety for them will never obscure the vision of what is highest and best, or absorb the energies of heart and mind to the exclusion of the truth and love of God. Life itself will be regarded as a subordinate thing, a means to an end, and that end the Kingdom of God. If it cannot be preserved without the doing of that which is alien to the Kingdom, it is not worth preserving. To the mind of Jesus existence is not " life." " My meat," He said, " is to do the will of My Father, who is in Heaven." There are some things which a man must not give to preserve existence, but nothing that he must not give to preserve his " life." We must read the sneer of Satan in the light of the thought of Jesus, and say, " All that a man hath will he give for his ' life ' "—the life of the soul—the life with God, in His Kingdom. What is of highest value is to be seen and held, it matters not at what cost. First things are to be placed first, and all secondary things will come after in their own proper order.

It is when this order is reversed that worldly things become dangerous, and that the souls of men are lost. When the treasures of the world with their immense attractiveness are regarded as the highest good, the blessedness of love and righteousness and communion with God is lost sight of. Men busy themselves with the Muck Rake, and are blind to the Crown of Life which is above them. The prizes of the world dazzle their eyes, and nothing else seems more desirable. Qualities of the soul, which would have found their development in riches toward God, are allowed to lie dormant, and possibilities of spiritual achievement remain unattempted. Not without meaning is it said, " Ye cannot serve God and Mammon." Wealth may become a god to men, so mighty is its influence, so seductive its attractiveness, so tremendous its power. It debases its worshippers, and destroys the soul that loves it. The love of money is " a root of all evil." It gives to riches the devotion which is due to God alone, and seeks its desire without much care as to the righteousness of the means which it employs. The corruptions of trade, the triumphs of " smartness," the oppression of the weak, the thousand countless acts of injustice and deceit which disgrace the life of the world, spring from the strength of its passion. The moral perspective of life is wrong. Wealth is put in the foreground as the real and only good worth seeking. The Kingdom of God with its righteousness and peace, and its communion with God, is lost sight of. Yet it is " by these things men live, and in them is the life of the spirit." Men

The First Things of Jesus

(as they seek the treasure which deludes them with its promise of good) hear not the question of Jesus, " What is a man advantaged if he gain the whole world and lose his own soul ? " The world needs nothing so urgently to-day as the power to see that the Kingdom of God is the real joy of the soul. Wealth must be looked at as Jesus saw it : its perils recognised as He recognised them. The social, economic and moral miseries of men persist, because His revelation of the true end of life is not accepted.

> " Lazarus hungry
> Menaces Dives,
> Labour, the giant,
> Chafes in his hold." *

The wealthy are dissatisfied and add luxury to luxury in vain. God hath set "eternity" in the heart of man, and nothing but eternal things can satisfy it.

But we must not imagine that it is only in the pursuit of wealth that the soul may be lost. It may also be lost in the effort to keep body and soul together. The worldly ideal may be cherished under rags as well as under fine raiment ; it may be the inspiration of the beggar as of the millionaire. The poor may starve the soul by anxiety for the things of the body. They may be so absorbed in

*Wm. Watson, " England My Mother."

the struggle to live that they forget the end for which life was given. The light and love of God may be hidden by the close pressure of physical need. Simply to keep body and soul together, men may yield to the temptations of dishonesty, or untruth. They may justify their wrong-doing by the thought that it is not done for wealth but for food, not for comfort or luxury, but for the preservation of life. Once again the sense of the true values of the temporal and the spiritual has been reversed. Life has been given up for existence. The soul has lost touch with God that it may keep in touch with the things needful for the body. Jesus says it is of more importance to keep God and the soul together than to keep body and soul together.

6. But, beyond that, He says that the anxiety for the lower needs of life is baseless and foolish. " Behold the fowls of the air " ; " Consider the lilies of the field." If God feeds the sparrow and clothes the lily, shall He not feed and clothe those who are made in His image and who do His will ? It is as if Jesus said, " Care for the things of God, and He will care for you." " Give the first thought to the doing of what will please Him, and He will not fail to provide for your necessities."

Jesus is asking men to do what He did Himself. He knew the numberless spiritual perils of poverty.* He suffered hunger, and had power to make the stones of the Wilderness bread. But to use His power in that way would have shown that He put self before God, and the satisfying of hunger before the interests of His Kingdom. He saw that " life was more than meat," that " man did not live by bread alone, but by every word that proceedeth out of the mouth of God." He set the Kingdom first, and the angels ministered unto Him. Because He was tempted thus He is able to succour those who are tempted by the same pressure of need. It is in divinest pity that He says to the poor " Seek ye first the Kingdom of God and His righteousness, and all these things shall be added unto you." He knew the tragedies of the souls of men, knew how the soul could be lost in the strong and urgent pressure of the demands of the body. Therefore He spoke so convincingly and so persuasively of the Heavenly Father's care, and gave the great assurance of His loving watchfulness. " To Him man's dearer than to himself."† He bids men trust God to provide what they need for the body,

* " Poverty is the greatest temptation that can fall in the way of men and women. Pray to be guarded against this temptation. Pray with all your heart and soul and strength for your daily bread. Poverty causes sins innumerable. Poverty destroys honour and self-respect. When the poor begin to fall they think to stay their fall by sin and crime. Poverty fills our prisons ; it turns honesty into crime, and virtue into dishonour."—W. BESANT, " The Bells of St. Paul's."

† Ben Jonson.

Seek First the Kingdom of God

and give their anxiety and strength to the doing
of His will. God will not deny Himself. Faithfulness on our part will be answered by faithfulness
on His.   His name has ever been " Jehovah-jireh " :
" The Lord will provide."   If men seek first the
Kingdom of God, He will not fail to add all " these
things."

The First Commandment

" For in two commandments are all the law
    And the prophets under the sun.
  And the first is last, and the last is first
    And the twain are verily one."—WHITTIER.

" What is the beginning ? Love. What is the
    course ? Love still.
  What is the goal ? The goal is Love, on the
    happy hill.
  Is there nothing then but Love, search we sky
    and earth ?
  There is nothing out of Love hath perpetual worth.
  All things flag but only Love, all things fail or flee.
  There is nothing left but Love worthy you and me.

  Lord give me Love, that I may love Thee much.
  Lord give me Love, that I may love Thee more."
                          CHRISTINA ROSSETTI.

    " Did Heaven vouchsafe some sign . . . .
      . Then might I read full clear
      E'en in my sensual prison,
        That Life and Law and Love are one
          symphonious name."
              W. WATSON, *Hope of the World*.

CHAPTER VIII

" THE FIRST COMMANDMENT "

ONE day in particular stands out in the Gospel history as the Day of Questions. On it Jesus made His last visit to the Temple and ended His public ministry. The Pharisees and Herodians came to Him, inquiring about the lawfulness of paying tribute to Cæsar ; the Sadducees followed with their ridiculous puzzle regarding the Resurrection ; and a lawyer, tempting Him, said, " Master, which is the great commandment in the Law ? " (Matt. xxii. 36). We do not see what temptation there was in the question. Even when we translate it more literally as " What kind of commandment is great in the Law ? " we fail to see the snare. But the Evangelist detected the hostile tone. Possibly the inquirer thought that, as Jesus was unaccustomed to the subtilties of Rabbinical casuistry, He might say something in reply which would provide a means of entanglement. It matters little what was in his mind, for Jesus did not give him the opportunity which he sought. He laid down no principle by which it could be determined what qualities made a commandment great.   He lifted the whole matter out of the arena of scholastic discussion.   He directed attention to the supreme duties which lie upon the conscience, and in regard to which there is no controversy.   " Thou shalt love the Lord thy God with all thy heart, and with all thy soul, and with all thy mind.   This is the first and great commandment ; and the second is like unto it, Thou shalt love thy neighbour as thyself.   On these two commandments hang all the Law and the Prophets."

I.   There is no originality in the words of the summary.   They belong to the Old Covenant, and are at least as old as the Pentateuch.   The originality lay in uniting the separated precepts, " Thou shalt love the Lord thy God," and " Love thy neighbour as thyself " ; in declaring that on these two "hang all the Law and the Prophets," and in giving them their unique pre-eminence as " first " and " second." Even if some nameless Jewish teacher, with clear prophetic insight, had done all this before, it was Jesus who gave the summary its currency and power. It matters much by whom words are spoken. The same tune may be played on a child's musical toy and a great cathedral organ, but what a difference there is in the rendering ! On the lips of Jesus the sum of the Law became

The First Commandment

a veritable word of life, thrilling the souls of men with its inspiration. Certain it is that these two commandments from the book of the Law had been neglected. No words were more familiar than those of the first, for they were repeated by every Jew night and morning from earliest boyhood, and were inscribed on the phylacteries which were so proudly worn by the Pharisees. But they had ceased to be words of living power. In that degenerate time, the " Sayings of the Elders " were regarded as " weightier than the Prophets." Rules of ritual were of more importance than such great duties. The jewels were not seen to be gems of priceless worth. Jesus rescued them from their obscurity, lifted them to honour, made them " sparkle on the finger of Time." Here, He said, is the whole duty of man ; this is his complete and perfect law of life : love embraces everything.

But the Pharisees, prepossessed with the idea that rules of ritual were of greatest moment, had their whole outlook on life darkened and confused. Trivialities were exalted to the highest place, to the exclusion or subordination of the weightier matters of the Law. They gave God ritual for righteousness, sacrifice for sanctity, obedience to a thousand and one petty precepts in place of love. Convention meant more to them than conscience. A low and unspiritual view of God lay at the bottom of their mistake. His essential holiness, mercy, goodness and truth were hidden from them. To them He was an infinite and perfect Pharisee. They thought to please Him by the multiplication of religious rites, and saw not that the Lord required them " to do justly and to love mercy, and to walk humbly with " Him (Micah vi. 8). Jesus set the duties of life in their true relation. Love came before everything.

2. Nothing makes religion so hurtful or so hateful as the working out of the pitiful conception that the forms and institutions of religion are of special worth in the sight of God. St. Peter, in speaking to plain men like himself, said it imposed a " yoke which neither our fathers nor we were able to bear " (Acts xv. 10). Wherever this conception becomes dominant, there is always a revolt against religion. The awful cry of Voltaire " *Ecrasze l'Infâme* " shocks us. We shudder to know that such words were applied to the Lord Jesus. But when we realise how deeply Christianity had become corrupted in Voltaire's day, we begin to understand the feelings which moved him to that dreadful utterance. Gambetta's famous political principle, " *Clericalisme, c'est l'ennemi,*" sprang from the same source, but was guided by a clearer discrimination between Christ and the Church which bore His Name.

The First Commandment

But in spite of all rebellion and apostasy, the first duty of man must ever be that which he owes to God. His place is absolute and alone. The creature must never be allowed to usurp the place of the Creator. The obligations of man to man will never be truly fulfilled, until the obligation which God requires is reverently and joyously accomplished. The inspiration and guidance of social service are only to be found in the hearty and faithful service of God. But that service must be rightly interpreted, and it is this which we have received from the Lord Jesus. It is summed up in the one word, love. Not rite, or ceremony, or sacrifice, but love.

3. It is one of the glories of revealed religion that it contains this commandment as the interpretation of the whole duty of man to God. The Old Testament has it as well as the New, but it was neglected till Jesus gave it prominence. We search in vain among other religions of the world for any rule of life like this. None of the gods whom men have worshipped has made such a demand on those who bowed at their shrines. Indeed, who could love Jupiter or Jaganath, or any of the deities represented by the ugly idols of heathendom? But the God of Abraham, Isaac and Jacob, the God and Father of our Lord and Saviour Jesus Christ, has required this from His worshippers that they

should love Him, for the duty is in harmony with His character.   Even in the beginning of revelation, when " He made known His ways unto Moses, His acts unto the children of Israel," it was seen that He was " merciful and gracious, slow to anger, and plenteous in mercy," and that " like as a father pitieth his children, so the Lord pitieth them that fear Him."   He commanded the Jews of the ancient time to love Him, because He was worthy to be loved.   And if it was so at the dawn of revelation, how much more reasonable is the commandment in the light of the perfect day of Christ ?   In the long gallery of human memory there is no more lovable character than that of Jesus Christ, and His revelation is enshrined in the marvellous saying, " He that hath seen Me hath seen the Father " (John xiv. 9).

4.   But men stumble at love to God being presented as a command.   They say love comes instinctively, without compulsion, as the outflow of feelings which are unconscious of their origin. The objection would be valid if the command to love God were simply an external enactment, on a level with the law " Thou shalt not kill."   But it is not a law imposed from without.   It speaks to something which lies beneath and above all the intellectual and moral activities.*   It is conditioned

* Dale, "Christian Doctrine," p. 182.

The First Commandment

by the character of God, the nature of man and the relations in which men stand to Him. Between a king and his subjects the relation is one in which loyalty is justly required, and it is joyfully rendered when the ruler is just and good. It might be objected with equal force that loyalty cannot be urged as a duty! There is nothing unreasonable in the apostolic precept that servants should " obey in all things their masters, not with eye-service as men-pleasers, but in singleness of heart fearing God " (Col. iii. 22). Such service is the only true fulfilment of the obligation which servants owe to masters, and if the latter are kind and considerate its enforcement is just and right. Husbands again are commanded to love their wives, because love is the essential condition on which marriage is founded. Love is simply a command to live together in accordance with the conditions and purposes which are implied in the relation of marriage. Love is its reason, its life and its law.

So the command to love God presupposes a personal relation which is both intimate and spiritual, and a nature in both of which love is an essential quality. It depends on the fundamental facts that God is lovable, that He loves us, and that we have the power of loving Him.

We cannot explain how love is born. Even between man and maid, love is one of the ultimate experiences of life which defy all analysis. It springs up of itself we know not how. We may say that there is knowledge, sympathy, or affinity, but beyond these there is a nameless something which acts, and love is born. It may come at first sight, or after years of intimacy. And it is the same with the love of man to God. It is the fulfilling of the relationship which exists between them. It comes we know not how. We do not explain its presence by saying that it arises out of knowledge, sympathy or affinity. We can only say " we love Him, because He first loved us " (1 John iv. 19), or that " the love of God is shed abroad in our hearts by the Holy Spirit which He hath given us " (Romans v. 5). But when once the relationship is realised, it is recognised that love is also its reason, its life and its law. When the love of God is known there is no difficulty in obeying the Commandments. It is the indication of His will that men should live in accordance with the character of the nature in which He created them. " Love the gift is Love the debt."*

It may be that we also require to emphasise the fact that men possess the power of loving God. We have been made in His image. Instincts have been implanted within us which can answer to the call of love. Love is the law of our life because

* Tennyson.

it is the end for which we were created. As long as it is not quickened, our nature is stunted and undeveloped. We know not what we are or can be ; life's meaning and glory are hidden from us until that love is born, and once born it can never die. We are unable to say if "love " is the perfect tense of " live," but if the etymology is wrong, there is no doubt about the fact that love is the perfection of life. " Everyone that loveth God hath been born of God and knoweth God," and to know Him is eternal life. " He that loveth not knoweth not God, for God is love." That is the penalty. The loveless soul is punished by its lovelessness. There is the insight of the genius of a Christian spirit in St. Teresa's saying about the demons, " How unhappy ! They do not love."

5. The command to love God includes and transcends all others. It strikes at the root of all disobedience. Sin is rebellion against God, but love restores the rebel to the light and joy of His face. Evil flows from the bitter spring of self-will, but love cleanses the fountain and makes the waters sweet. Fear is the result of sin, but " perfect love casteth out fear." God is served as a trustful child obeys its father. Where there is love there is no need for law. Our legislature has passed laws of various kinds to compel parents to feed, clothe and educate their children, and to hinder

them from cruelty, but in how many homes are these laws unneeded and unknown? In the largest and fullest sense, St. Paul's great words are true, " Love is a fulfilling of Law." We can even accept the daring words of Augustine when he said, " Love God, and do what you like." It is not only that the restraints of love are absolute, holding us back from evil, and overcoming all unworthy affections when all checks of other kinds have broken down, but its inspirations and guidance are equally complete. It is equipped with a wisdom which the reason does not know, armed with weapons which the world cannot fashion, and strengthened with a power which finds its unfailing source in God. Nothing escapes from its sway. It permeates the whole of life and subdues all things to itself.

So also where there is love there is liberty. The law may be holy and just and good, but it is still law, and presents itself in the stern and august aspects of restraint. It must be transfused and transformed by love, if its essential character is to be changed. The Law-giver must be seen behind the law; the Personality behind the principle; and not only seen but loved, before this transformation can be effected. Law can never lay aside its terrors and penalties, but when the face of the Father is seen, and His tender voice is heard, the law becomes the Father's Will. It is not a burden but a blessing, not a categorical imperative but a perpetual inspiration. Love supplies both knowledge and strength. God's statutes are as songs in the night. If it is true that "licht is the burden love lays on," it is equally true that " licht" is the burden love takes up. " His commandments are not grievous."

Sin is still a possibility, for love may be imperfect. The lover of God may still be saddened by omissions, transgressions, failures, shortcomings, but even imperfect love will keep a man from conscious and continued sins. There will, however, be no self-righteous contentment or ignorant claim to perfection in his heart. The consciousness of sin may become deeper as life and love go on together. The loving soul may still have to cry the prayer of the penitent, " God be merciful to me, a sinner." But the sins of wilfulness will cease. " What the law could not do because of the weakness of the flesh," the love which has been shed abroad in his heart will enable him to accomplish. All things are possible to him that loveth.

6. But our duty is not ended till we love intensely," with all the heart and with all the soul, and with all the mind." The duty is to become a passion, the fire is to burn to a flame. We have not loved enough till we love with all our powers. We may miss the emphasis of this high duty of loving with

our utmost energy, if we consider too minutely the separate clauses in which it is expressed. Heart and soul and mind have no actual separateness in the life of man. The repeated phrases are only intended to indicate with emphasis the completeness with which every power within us is to be active in the love of God. If any stress is laid upon them, they can only be regarded as describing slightly different aspects of the energy of love.

" *Love with all thy heart.*" We think of the heart as the seat of the emotions, the fountain of feeling and desire, the hearth where the fire burns which gives warmth to our affections. The love of the heart is instinctive. It knows not whence it comes or whither it goes. It asks no explanation and demands no proofs. It is its own witness and its own warrant. With all the force and passion of this instinctive power, we are to love the Lord our God.

" *Love with all thy soul.*" This is the love of choice or preference, of admiration or adoration. It is conscious of itself and can give reasons for its existence. It is more than sentiment or feeling. It is the glad perception of truth, beauty and goodness ; the willing trust and choice of God as worthy of our devotion. In an especial degree it is the love that can be commanded. It has knowledge as its foundation, reverence as its dominant quality, faith and appreciation as its quickening powers. It is the response of the soul to the vision of excellence, the delight in the perfections of God. With all the power of this spiritual recognition and choice of excellence, we are to love God.

"*Love with all thy mind.*" The love of God is not to be "blind." Knowledge is to illuminate it, and be the source of its increasing strength and joy. The more we know of the word and works and character of God, the more reverent and whole-hearted will our love become. Some one has said, "What is perfect love, but perfect knowledge." There is no opposition between the knowledge and the love of God. The love of God never suffers from knowledge, but from the lack of it. When Jesus repeated this injunction, He consecrated the activity of all the intellectual powers. If it is true, as Pasteur suggested, that the *débacle* of Sedan had its hidden cause in the neglect of thought among the French, it is much more true that the failure of faith and love in the Church and the Christian is to be traced very frequently to the same source. Not with impunity does any Church or Christian allow the powers of the mind to remain unexercised. Slackness of mental energy, dread of knowledge in any form, are the worst enemies of faith and love. Therefore with all the powers of mind we must love the Lord our God.

7.   If this commandment is obeyed to the full we shall not neglect the word which says " Thou shalt love thy neighbour as thyself." The second commandment is like the first. It sets forth love as the sum of man's duty to man, embracing it within the Golden Rule, bidding us put ourselves in the place of our neighbour and give him the love we would wish for ourselves. The " second " is really the offspring of the " first." As the brotherhood of man arises from the Fatherhood of God, so love to man finds its only source in the love of God. Jesus puts the two commands together, linking them in thought and word lest they should be separated. The inspiration of the love of man is found in the love of God, that is, morality is inspired by religion. The love of God is interpreted by the love of man, that is, religion is preserved from formalism by morality. In the first commandment we have the sum and substance of all religion ; in the second the sum and substance of all morality,* and they cannot live apart from one another. " He that loveth God " will " love his brother also."

* Denney, *Expositor*, Fifth Series, vol. iii, p. 318.

Whosoever will be First

" We seek to mount the still ascending stair
Of greatness, glory, and the crowns they bear,
We mount to fall self-sickened in despair,
The purposes of life misunderstood
Baffle and wound us, but God only would
That we should heed His simple words, ' Be Good.' "

" It takes us a long time and a sharp discipline
to learn that he who would keep his life must lose it,
and that to empty oneself is the sure way to be filled.
The heart of man is so constituted that its fulness
comes from spending. In the great things of life
Christianity has taught us this sublime lesson, but
it is applicable to the lesser things of life. When
we serve we rule. When we give we have. When
we surrender ourselves we are victors. We are
most ourselves when we lose sight of ourselves. We
know not what we are or what we may be. As the
seed has a tree in it so men have within them angels."

JOHN H. NEWMAN.

" The world knows nothing of its greatest men."

SIR HENRY TAYLOR, *Philip van Artevelde*.

CHAPTER IX

" WHOSOEVER WILL BE FIRST "

No question interested the companion-disciples of Jesus so much as this, " Which of them would be the greatest in the Kingdom of Heaven ? " They were ready to discuss it at all times. Even when Jesus was burdened with the thought of His death, this was the matter about which they were concerned. They believed that the Kingdom, so long foretold, so eagerly expected, was near at hand. Every hope that the Jews cherished was to be fulfilled. Jerusalem was to be the capital of a great world state. Jesus was to be the Messiah Prince, and they as His chosen followers were certain to have high office and place within it. Had it not been said that they would " sit on twelve thrones judging the twelve tribes of Israel ? " Perhaps as is usual among ourselves before a general election, the various offices of state had been distributed beforehand. Judas Iscariot would, of course, be the Chancellor of the Exchequer ! But who was to be the Prime Minister—the man next to the king ?   That was the position for which there were many aspirants.   Discuss its occupancy as they might, the question could not be definitely settled by the disciples.   It came up again without result ; no one was willing to yield to the other. The interest which it excited may be measured by the fact, that when Salome made the request that her two sons, James and John, might sit the one on the right hand and the other on the left of Jesus in His Kingdom, the other ten disciples were indignant.   They thought that she and they were wishing to take an unfair advantage over them.

As this matter came up frequently in the minds of the disciples, our Lord often repeated His teaching in regard to it.   He had other thoughts than they of the character of His Kingdom, and other ideas of the highest place within it, and of how it was to be reached.   It was not a Kingdom of this world as the disciples imagined.   Greatness within it was of another kind than that of which they dreamed, and was to be secured by means which had never occurred to them.   The honours which men seek were as nothing to the honours which He saw. In His Kingdom the prizes were to be found where the world never looked for them.   So He called them to Him and said, " Whosoever will be great among you, let him be your minister, and whosoever

Whosoever will be First

will be first among you, let him be your slave "
(Matt. xx. 26-27).

1. We notice that our Lord does not condemn
the desire to be " first." In His thought ambition
is not an evil power.

We point to the evils which ambition has wrought,
and name many a warrior and statesman as
warnings of its baleful influence. But our Lord
does not do so. He leaves room in the life of His
disciples for the exercise of this elemental passion.
It is said to be " the last infirmity of noble minds,"
and even a little child who says " me first!" is moved
by it. But Jesus does not regard it as an infirmity.
It is a power, with which God has endowed our
nature, without which we should be poor and un-
aspiring. The desire to excel is simply the desire
to be first. It is the spring of energy ; the spur of
effort. Jesus is too wise to check the instinct by
which men seek to lift themselves higher. He
sanctifies all the powers of our nature ; He destroys
none of them. It is complete men whom He
desires, not emasculated creatures from whom the
distinctive qualities of manhood have been taken.
They are to " covet earnestly the best gifts," and
strive for the first place. Behind all achievement
there is the desire to attain. Therefore Jesus does
not condemn the desire. He would encourage
men to seek the first place, but He gives them a new

perspective. He throws the light of His knowledge on the real life of men when He shows what the first place is, and how it is to be reached.

2. His thought of it is one that still surprises us, as it no doubt surprised the disciples who heard of it from His lips. Like the rest of men they thought that the chief place was at the top of the social ladder. Jesus says it is at the bottom. " If any man desire to be first, the same shall be last of all," " Whosoever will be first among you, let him be your slave." The world's first is His last ; its last is His first. High station, great offices in which men rule over others, and have many to serve or tremble at their word, are the chief positions measured by the judgment of the world. The throne is its symbol of greatness. But to Jesus the place of the servant, even of the slave, is the type of the highest. Men are accustomed to say that there is always plenty of room at the top, that the crush of the crowd is at the bottom. All are striving for a step upwards on the social ladder ; to them the heights are above. But to Jesus the highest place is at the bottom, from which all are seeking to escape !

This reversal of first and last is one of the distinctive ideas of Jesus. By this word He accomplished part of His great redemptive work for human kind. He lifted the stigma of service, the shame of meanness, the degradation of labour, from the toiling millions of the earth. The first place is that which men think lowest of all. He reached it when He was lifted to the Cross, where, in the fulness of His service, He gave His life for the world. In Heine's dream the old divine rulers of men faded away into nothingness when the pale figure of the Crucified, staggering under the weight of the Cross, came in amongst them. " He humbled Himself and became obedient unto death, even the death of the cross," and it became His throne. He " reigns from the Tree." When His foes placed Him there, they thought that they were degrading Him beneath human memory, but they really exalted Him to be first of all. It is the Lamb—symbol of lowliness, weakness, and tenderness—" slain from the foundation of the world," that is exalted to the Throne of Heaven.

3. The Lord's way of attaining to the first place is equally surprising. The world holds that greatness is to be measured by the number of those over whom authority is exercised. Its emblems of power are the " Sceptre, the Sword, the Eagle, the Leopard, and the Lion—Rods of Iron, and Beasts and Birds of Prey." There is truth in the keen satire of Landor, that " Whoever wishes to be thought great among men must do them some great mischief, and the longer he continues doing things of this sort,

the more he will be admired."* Jesus says, greatness is to be measured by service, by the number of good deeds which one can do to others. It was an idea so startling and unexpected that He points to His own life as its illustration. He says, " I am among you as one that serveth." " The picture of the Man girt with the linen towel affects me more " (someone has said) " than Sinai wrapt in smoke." To Him the weakness and necessities of men were not opportunities of taking advantage of them, but of serving and helping them. Without money and without price to others, He helped the helpless, and " took upon Him their infirmities and sicknesses." His life is summed up in the briefest of biographies, " He went about doing good." The Name of Jesus has become the most glorious name in all the world, but how did it gather around it such imperishable fame ? When He lived in Palestine, there were many who bore the name of Jesus. The very robber whom the people preferred to Him was known as " Jesus Barabbas ! " Why is it that the Name of Jesus of Nazareth is above every other name ? There is no answer but this—" He made Himself of no reputation, He took upon him the form of a servant; He became obedient unto death even the death of the cross. Wherefore God also hath highly exalted Him and given Him a name

* " Imaginary Conversations," vol. ii., p. 63.

which is above every name, that in the name of
Jesus every knee should bow, of things in heaven,
and things in earth, and things under the earth."
Jesus became first of all because He became servant
of all. His position was higher than that of the
kings of the world, but He used it that He might
be the Servant of men, the Saviour of sinners. His
powers were vaster than those which men possess,
but He consecrated them all to the service of men.
He counted not His equality with God as a thing to
be prized ; He prided not Himself on the powers
which He could exercise. All His gifts were gifts
for men.

And this is how He would have men regard
themselves and all that they possess. Position in
the world, social influence, money, talents, powers
of mind and heart, are simply capacities and instruments to use aright or to misuse. The more a man
has the more he may do. Our possessions are
never ours alone ; they are ours for use. We never
know the possibilities of help or joy which are
within our reach, until we follow the way of Jesus,
and regard ourselves as put in trust with the things
we call our own. Then we can indulge to the full
the desire to be first. Ambition finds its true
exercise and field of operation. It is cleansed
from all self-seeking, and redeemed from the
hardness which otherwise clings to it. " To do

good hoping for nothing again " is its joy and reward.

4.   Such teaching still sounds somewhat strangely in the ears of men. Christ's example and precepts receive but scant attention in the Church, to say nothing of the world. His disciples are still as unready to follow Him in this way of greatness as the first disciples were. We need to have the lesson repeated again and again, even as they did. Yet He *has* moved the world by His words and life. The great men of the pre-Christian era—what is the secret of their fame ? Heaps of skulls perpetuate the name of Tamerlane ; military conquests preserve the names of Alexander and Cæsar. Tyrants were euphemistically named " benefactors." Of these we can repeat the words of Horace Walpole, " How many must be wretched before one can be renowned ! "   We do not refer to Plato or Aristotle, or even to Socrates, for illustrations of the greatness which Jesus has taught us to admire and follow, (though we do not suggest that these were not servants of mankind or that by their works they did not render incalculable benefits to men), for they loved truth rather than humanity, and lacked the motive which distinguishes and inspires the service which Christ would have us give. The poor were beyond their view, and the thought of helping them did not press upon their hearts. But since Jesus

lived and taught, a new spirit and a new activity are discernible, however faint at times are the signs of their presence. He has lifted up what the ancient world suppressed. The saints of the Christian Church, unless in times of perverted views of holiness, have ever been lovers and servants of men. There are still great men of the old pagan type like Napoleon, Moltke, and Bismarck, but their glory is dim compared with that which shines around the dearer names of Howard, Lincoln, Wilberforce, and Livingstone. Even in the domain of Science, however great have been the material blessings which have come from the discoveries of men who are honoured with undying fame, it is those whose service has affected the ills that " flesh is heir to," who receive the highest honours. The names of Newton and Kepler and Darwin are not so dear to the heart of the world as those of Simpson, Pasteur, and Lister. So, too, the motto of the Prince of Wales " Ich Dien ; " the title of the Pope, " Servus Servorum ; " and the name of the chief of the Cabinet, " the Prime Minister," are indications of the effect of the teaching and example of Jesus, even if these phrases have little effect on life and conduct. It is now widely recognised that a place in our national Valhalla is the peculiar honour of those who by their life and works have gladdened and sweetened human life. " We do not bury our millionaires in

The First Things of Jesus

Westminster Abbey." It is not possessions which make men great in the estimate of Jesus. It is the use they make of them. Christ did most for men because He possessed most. "He was rich and for our sakes became poor, that we through His poverty might be made rich." He gave Himself, and therefore won His glorious Name. And the best gifts are always found in that way. They give most who only give themselves.

5. And it is not only the teaching and example of Jesus, which give us the assurance that the way to the highest place is by service. As we think over the experience of Christian life, we can see many reasons which add their force to His instructions. The service of others secures the first place because it alone wins love and trust. In the story of the Crimean War, the one name which shines with a growing lustre is that of Florence Nightingale, " the lady with the lamp." A king whose name is on the lips of millions may be detested, and a great sigh of relief may come from them when death removes him. A peasant may be a real prince among men, because of the little nameless unremembered acts of kindness and of love which endear him to his native village. The mightiest power of the world is in the hands of those who spend themselves in helping others. It is they who can awaken the hope of pardon in the hearts of the vilest ; who can cheer the degraded

Whosoever will be First

with the possibilities of recovery ; who can keep
alive the spark of faith in the Divine goodness, in
lives which have been overwhelmed by calamity
and distress. The most honoured names upon the
roll of earthly fame, are the names of the servants
of men. The monuments which evoke the greatest
reverence are those which love and gratitude have
built. The servant of all makes for himself a place
which is peculiarly his own. The throne of a king
has always an heir-apparent, ready to step into the
vacant place, but he who lives that he may serve
leaves a blank which none can fill. Greatness as
well as " wisdom is ofttimes nearer when we stoop
than when we soar."

The world is full of the tragedy of disappointment,
change and loss regarding all that it calls " great."
When the coronation ceremony which made
Napoleon I Emperor of the French was over, the
newly-made ruler cast his robes from him with the
cry, " I have never spent a more tiresome day."
And the place he gained at such a cost of misery to
millions he could not keep. His vast ambitions
massed against him the conscience and the powers
of Europe, and men felt as if a dark eclipse had
passed from the sun when he was exiled to St.
Helena. The vanity of riches, the vicissitudes of place
and power are the commonplaces of history. " Success," said one who won it, " is a hideous thing."

But the men and women who have followed the way of Christ declare with one voice the joy and peace and fulness of the life of service. Nothing gladdens like goodness ; nothing abides like loving kindness ; nothing gives the sense and glory of completeness to the life of man like the ministry of helpfulness.

Then also this way of life makes the man himself great. It is not severed from character ; it issues in character. The honours of the world are outside things, which may be worn like decorations, and may be torn from the breast in a moment. They have no essential relation to the character of the man who wears them. The crown of earthly power may rest on the head of a Nero, but the man who serves his kind gains a nobility of nature which lifts him higher than the kings of the earth. " The reward of virtue is virtue." At the last estimate of greatness, it is goodness which wins the crown of life.

6. May it not also be said that the way of service shows its value because it opens the path of greatness to every one ? The winners of the prizes of the world must always be few. Thrones, dominions, riches, knowledge, are possible only to a tiny number amid the vast crowds of men, and are often misused, or abused. They are not the mightiest powers. But the poorest and humblest of mankind can serve.

Whosoever will be First

The lowliest lot is as near the way of greatness as the highest. Is there poverty or ignorance or sorrow near us ? Can we comfort the mourner, cheer the downcast, help the helpless, lift the fallen ? Wherever the loving hand can be stretched out to serve, or the tender word of sympathy can be spoken, there are little lowly doors into the way of greatness. Even those who are burdened with the loss of faculties find that it is open to them. " I thank God," said Dr. Moon, " for my talent of blindness."

The world may ignore the followers of the lowly way of Jesus, but it is enough for the disciple that he be as His Lord.

It did not know Him when He walked among men, and it may not see the greatness of those who seek to do His will and share in His ministering spirit. Jesus has taught us that it is not the recognition of men which awards the glory of life, and it is not even the result that wins it. The motive is everything. If we can do the humblest acts of service as unto Him, true greatness and dignity of soul are assured to us. Nothing can be menial or low which is done according to His desire, or in obedience to His will. The servants who serve Him are made as " kings and priests unto God." The world may never honour them, but He who " causeth the sun to rise on the evil and the good, and the rain to descend on the just and the unjust,"

will not despise their humble efforts to do good.
" He that humbleth himself shall be exalted, yea
the Lord shall lift him up." He will know them
though the world never may.

" The light shineth in darkness, and the darkness
comprehendeth it not." " He came unto His
own, and His own received Him not, but as many
as received Him to them gave He power to become
the sons of God—even to them that believe on His
name"—and that is in truth to be " first of all."

The First shall be Last, and the Last First

"It is a sign of moral health that men have so largely ceased to be interested in the question of rewards and punishments."

G. A. Coe, The Religion of a Mature Mind.

"The reward of duty done is the power to do another."—George Eliot.

"Heaven rejects the lore
Of nicely calculated less or more."

Wordsworth, King Henry's Chapel.

"The noblest and the best
Are those of whom we never knew,
God's greatest are God's lowliest,
Who moved unnoted to their rest,
Nor built their pride on human woe."

The Outcast.

"Your reward or soon or late
Will come from Him whom no man serves in vain."

Browning, Paracelsus.

CHAPTER X

"THE FIRST SHALL BE LAST, AND THE LAST FIRST"

In the closing year of our Lord's ministry He appears to have thought much of the waste of opportunity, the misuse of privilege, and the reversal of human conditions and judgments in the light of the Kingdom of God. To His clear eye things were not what they seemed. Men were living in a mist of false estimates, in which all true values were lost. A boundless pity filled His heart as He looked out on the petty pride of men.

1. A vast gulf separated two classes of people in Palestine at that time. None was so highly honoured or so greatly favoured as the priest or the elder. Every social power or benefit belonged to them. Education, reputation, position, wealth distinguished them, and lifted them up to general admiration and esteem. In the grading of Jewish social life, the priest and Pharisee stood first, without dispute. At the opposite extreme were the publicans and harlots—men and women of no reputation, the outcasts of society, the very shame of Israel.

The First Things of Jesus

Nothing seemed more assured than that it was well with the priests and the Pharisees, and ill with the publicans and harlots. So the world judged and said. But Jesus saw something which the world did not see, and came to another conclusion. In the one class there was a haughty self-righteousness, an intolerable pride, a deeply-seated self-confidence, which made them unwilling to enter the humble door of the Kingdom of God. Their worldly privileges barred the way to the highest spiritual good of the time. The grace and truth of the Kingdom of God were of no value or interest to them. They saw no beauty in its Prince that they should desire Him. They hid as it were their faces from Him. They refused His call, and scorned His message. But the men and women whom they despised found in Him a strong attraction. He did not ignore them or despair of them. He treated them as men and women, lost children of God whom He had come to save, and spoke words which thrilled them with the hope of newness of life. As they listened to Him and marked His doings, many of them turned with loathing from their evil ways, and pressed with trembling eagerness into the Kingdom of God. They discovered that their sins and social disabilities did not bar them out. The blessings of the gracious Gospel were open to them, and they seized them with gladness. One of them even became a personal companion of the Messiah. Therefore Jesus said to the chief priests and elders of the people, " The publicans and harlots go into the Kingdom of God before you." Not yet was the great principle of reversal spoken, but here was its germ. The last were first and the first were last.

2. As time went on, this reversal of human conditions was seen to be working in a wider sphere. The world was then divided into Jews and Gentiles. To the one belonged age-long privileges, peculiar revelations, special blessings—" the adoption and the glory, and the covenants, and the giving of the Law, and the service of God, and the promises, whose also were the fathers, and of whom concerning the flesh Christ came " (Romans ix. 4, 5). No words are strong enough to express the extent and greatness of the advantage of the Jews. They regarded themselves as the favourites of heaven. They treated the Gentiles with contempt. These were the " uncircumcised," the " unclean," the " dogs " who were " without." Nothing was more certain to them than that it was good to be a Jew, and evil to be a Gentile. But Jesus foresaw the awful tragedy, the tremendous revolution, which was to take place. The Jews were to deny the faith in which they had lived, and destroy the hope which they had passionately cherished. The Desire of all Israel had come, and Israel had received Him

not. The rejection of the Messiah was to lead to their own rejection. They did not know the time of their visitation. Their house was to be left desolate. Their pride and privileges were to be crushed in the ruin of their State. But under the thick darkness of the doom which impended broodingly over Israel, Jesus saw on every horizon the eager rush of the Gentiles. They who could say, " We have eaten and drunk in Thy presence, and Thou hast taught in our streets " would be " thrust out," and those whom they had despised " would come from the east and from the west, and from the north and from the south, and sit down in the Kingdom of God." It is in connection with this amazing tragedy that the words were first spoken : " Behold, there are last which shall be first, and there are first which shall be last " (Luke xiii. 30.).

3. In this connection these words express a truth for all time. Men still walk in a vain show and know not their real condition. It is a constant danger that privileges may be lost, that opportunities may be wasted, and that those who are dowered with many advantages may be surpassed by those whom they despise. There are representatives of the divided classes of Palestine among us still ; the distinctions which separated Jews and Gentiles continue ; but we name them differently. They distinguish Christian from heathen countries ; they

separate the depraved and the respectable in society. The first in the judgment of the world may be last in the judgment of Christ. Nations and individuals have to stand at His bar, and may experience a great surprise when they hear His sentence. Those who are exalted into heaven may be cast down to hell, while the lowly and the sinful may be found lifted up to salvation and praise. The moral and respectable do not always please God by repentance and faith. The delusions of pride and self-righteousness may cling to them, and conceal from them the way of life. The privileges of Christian knowledge and training are not enough to bring men into the Kingdom of God. At best they are only opportunities. They secure that Christ is brought near, and brought near in the earliest days of life, but they may be misused. The needs of the soul may never be felt ; the glory of Christ may never be seen. Morality may take the place of religion, and trust in a good life may hide the need of faith in Christ. There is an austerity in the judgment of Christ which should make the lofty humble, and on the other hand there is a tenderness also which should make the depraved and the degraded hopeful. Hard conditions of life, and the burden and shame of sin, are not enough to shut out any soul from the mercy that is in Christ. The poor who have never been dazzled by worldly advantages, and the depraved who have never deceived themselves as to their sins, may be nearer the Kingdom of God than many a church-goer. The recurrence of the blindness of the priest and the Pharisee, the repetition of the tragedy of Israel's rejection, are always possible—the first may be last and the last first.

4. But this principle, which is seen working in relation to entrance into the Kingdom of God, also applies to rewards in its service. Our Lord's treatment of the rich young ruler had evidently surprised His disciples. Jesus had said to him, " Sell that thou hast and come, follow Me " (Matt. xix. 21). One inducement had been held out to him to counterbalance such a sacrifice. It was said that he would have " treasure in heaven." It may have been because St. Peter felt that this was a very unsubstantial recompense that, when the young man went away, he came to Jesus, saying, " Behold, we have left all and followed Thee ; what shall we have therefore ? " Were they also to have nothing but " treasure in heaven " ? Were all their substantial sacrifices to be recompensed in such visionary coin ? Was the Kingdom of God for which they were working, and for which they had left all, not an actual worldly reality ? Why should the Master say nothing about its glories to the young ruler, but speak only of " treasure in heaven ? " Was

The First shall be Last

it possible that the disciples had nothing more substantial to expect in return for all that they had given up ? This doubt must be cleared up at once, so he asked " What shall we have therefore ? "

Jesus answered him according to the condition of his mind in relation to spiritual things. He said, " Verily I say unto you, that ye who have followed Me, in the regeneration when the Son of Man shall sit in the throne of His glory, ye also shall sit upon twelve thrones, judging the twelve tribes of Israel; and every one that hath forsaken houses, or brethren, or sisters, or father or mother, or wife or children, or lands, for My name's sake, shall receive an hundredfold, and shall inherit eternal life. But many that are first shall be last, and the last shall be first " (Matt. xix. 28-30). In Mark, the details of sacrifice are repeated almost verbatim in the assurance of the recompense, and indicate the fact that the disciples understood the words of Jesus in their literal sense. But we cannot think that they are to be taken literally, or even figuratively, as if expressing the assurance that, through the sympathy and kindness of the Christian brotherhood, all that the disciples had left would be found again in fuller measure. Jesus is speaking to St. Peter and the disciples as one speaks to a child. They were at that stage of spiritual experience, when the certainty of reward could only be made real to them through material imagery. Our Lord might have said then, as He said at a later time, " I have many things to say unto you, but ye cannot bear them now." He gave them the assurance that the recompense of their sacrifice was certain and abundant in the only form in which it could be received by them, leaving it to time and experience to purify and elevate their desires.

5. But with the assurance of recompense the process of education begins. The selfish and bargaining spirit manifested by St. Peter was rebuked. He must not expect that the rewards of following Christ are to be in accordance with his personal expectations. The principle of rewards in the Kingdom of God is not " so much for so much." He is warned that the last may be first, and the first may be last. The parable of the labourers in the vineyard (Matt. xx. 1-16) is added to illustrate this point.

In many respects it is a most perplexing and bewildering parable, but its difficulties are avoided in large measure when we link it with our Lord's answer to St. Peter's question, and keep strictly to its main intention. Whatever other lessons the parable contains, its reference to the education of St. Peter must be its chief burden. It certainly illustrates the truths, that in the Kingdom of God rewards are not in accordance with personal

The First shall be Last

expectations, and that the last may be first and the first last. One principle runs through the parable, that the reward or recompense of all the workers is determined entirely by the will of the Master. Even the wage of the labourers who were first sent into the vineyard is settled by Him. They only knew what the wage would be. The length or severity of their toil gave them no right of complaint or claim against the Master. He gave them what He had promised to them, and was not to be hindered from giving the same to whomsoever He pleased. So the disciples who had been called into the service of the Kingdom of God in the early morning were chosen by Him. They had known the terms of their recompense from the beginning. In one form or another it had been described to them again and again. It had just been detailed once more in the great promise of an hundred-fold reward. With not a little humour it was now likened to a penny a day! But their length of service gave them no claim to more than they had been promised. Their Lord had promised that to them, and He was entirely free to treat others as He had treated them. If He gave as much to one who laboured only for an hour, what could be said but that it was His will? By the grace of that will the first may be last and the last first. St. Paul had grasped this great principle when he said, " So it is not of him that willeth or of him that runneth, but of God that showeth mercy." We notice the working of the same thought in our Lord's answer to the sons of Zebedee, when they came with the request that they might have the seats on the right hand and the left in the Kingdom of the Messiah. The promise that the disciples would sit on twelve thrones was evidently in their minds. But they wanted the chief seats on either side of the King. Jesus said to them " To sit on My right hand or on My left is not mine to give, but it shall be given to them for whom it is prepared of My Father " (Matt. xx. 23). The principle of the parable is again illustrated here. Rewards and recompenses are determined by His will.

Other parables may be studied for what they can tell us of the working of that gracious will, but it is its unhindered supremacy and unlimited freedom which are here asserted. It judges by other knowledge and standards than those which are available for us. We humbly strive to understand what they are and to judge ourselves by them. We also seek to make allowances for error in our verdicts upon the lives of others. We say God judges by the motive and not by the appearance, by the spirit and not by the action, by the intention and not by the achievement. He is not misled by circumstances or confused by worldly differences. He takes note not only of what men are, but of what they started with, what they fought with, and what strength of moral endeavour they put into the battle. Where much has been given, much is required. Faithfulness in little is equal to faithfulness in much. These are some of the things which we see in the working of the judgment of God, but they do not tell us everything. "Thy judgments are a great deep." But they are righteous, and true, and gracious. The more we know of them the more are we humbled in our own sight, and the more does the thought of merit before Him fade from our minds. We come to recognise the truth of what Jesus taught His disciples, that rewards and recompenses are entirely in His hand, and are purely the effluence of His grace.

6. It is remarkable to notice how large a place the idea of reward has in the teaching of Jesus. An exaggerated unworldliness would remove it entirely from the motives of the Christian life. A mistaken estimate as to the place and value of " good works " has degraded the conception of reward, until God's gracious purpose of salvation has become little better than a commercial transaction. But the mistakes of men are not to hide from us the fact that Jesus holds out the prospects of reward to all who serve Him. It is not the reward of merit, determined by our thoughts of what we should receive. It

The First Things of Jesus

is a reward of grace, determined by His will, and in every case it will be far above what we ask or think. There will be many surprises at the end ; human judgments will often be reversed ; the last will be first, it may be, and the first last. But in every case the reward will be of grace, and be determined by the great Master's will. He would have us to be free from a selfish and bargaining spirit ; He would deliver us from complaint and jealousy, have us enter into the joy of our Lord in the glad day when He calls His labourers home to their rest and reward.

First of all, Beware of Hypocrisy

"Since the establishment of Christianity as a state religion, the most stringently-framed oaths have never prevented an unscrupulous infidel from attaining any position that lay within reach of his wits and his opportunities. He has sat in the most orthodox Parliaments, he has been admitted to cabinet councils, he has worn royal crowns, he has even received the mitre, the Cardinal's hat, and the Papal tiara. We can never sufficiently admire the beautiful order of society by which the heretic-plus-liar is so graciously admitted everywhere, and the heretic-plus-honest-man is so cautiously and ingeniously kept out."—HAMERTON, *Human Intercourse*.

" To the lust of office and greed of praise
A stepping-stone is the altar made."
WHITTIER, *The Preacher*.

" 'Tis a spot as yet, but it will break
Into a hideous blotch if overlooked."
R. BROWNING, *Paracelsus*.

" Sincerity is the end and beginning of all things ; without sincerity there would be nothing."
CONFUCIUS.

CHAPTER XI

"FIRST OF ALL, BEWARE OF . . . HYPOCRISY"*

"Some sins," says the Westminster Shorter Cate-
chism, "are more heinous in the sight of God
than others." The principle also holds good in the
sight of man. The moral distinctions, however,
are not always the same. There are strange per-
versities and variations in the estimates of guilt
which men make. The standard varies with
land and age, and even with the class and the
individual. Our Lord introduced a new and permanent judgment of sin. He surprises us by His
tenderness, and severity, and by the evils against
which His condemnation is specially directed.
Jesus passed by the open vices of the world; drunkenness receives no rebuke; the "crimson sins" of
men are seldom noticed. He brought to the bar
of His judgment evils which were little or lightly
thought of by the general conscience. He had
a "Book of Strange Sins"! He was most compassionate and hopeful towards the outcasts of

* Margin of Revised Version, Luke xii. 1.

society, most severe towards those who were popularly revered and admired. His judgment began with the house of God. It is a fact never to be forgotten that the Pharisees—the representative men of the Church of that time—were sinners above all others to Him. They were the only class which He openly and sternly denounced. He differed from them in His conception of righteousness, and therefore of necessity differed from them in His conception of sin. To the Pharisees ceremonial uncleanness was the chief sin, a breach of the Sabbath law was a serious offence, failure to tithe mint and anise and cummin was a matter of graver importance than the omission of judgment, mercy and faith. In proverbial phrase, " They strained out the gnat and swallowed the camel " (Matt. xxiii. 24).

According to the moral perspective of Jesus, the sins of men were arranged in a widely different order from theirs. He set hypocrisy in the foreground as the sin of sins, while they had no place for it, or one that was so far away that it was almost lost to sight in the distance. It was the chief charge that He brought against the rulers of the people in the matters of religion. Their hypocrisy was hateful to Him. Their good works were many ; their precepts were admirable ; their zeal was praiseworthy ; but all their virtues were vitiated by the

First of all, Beware of Hypocrisy

low selfishness of their motives. They concealed
a worldly spirit and sometimes an evil life under
the seemly guise of a severe morality. The terrible
" Woes " of the twenty-third chapter of St. Matthew's
Gospel are an extended condemnation of their inconsistencies. The intensity of feeling with which that
condemnation is charged is the proof—if proof
is necessary—that to the mind of Jesus there was
no sin like hypocrisy. He would save " His own "
from its subtle and soul-destroying influences.
Therefore He gave them emphatic warning against
it : He said, " First of all, beware of hypocrisy."
In its grosser and simpler forms this sin may not be
as common now as it was in that far-off time. The
warnings of Jesus, His awful exposures of the sin,
His biting irony, have made it odious, but we dare
not say that it has been destroyed. It is the sin
which follows religion as the shadow follows the
sun. It permeates social life also, but its special
home is the sphere of religion.

In the old Greek world "hypocrite " was the
name of an actor. On the stage he wore a mask
which made him appear other than he really was.
He might strut about as a warrior or a king, while
he was but a poor coward or a simple peasant.
In this sense of " actor," the word is not found in
Scripture, but it is frequently used, figuratively,
to describe those who are living a life that is incon-

sistent with their professions. Religion has created certain forms and habits of life which are helpful or essential to its existence. The forms can be observed without the living spirit for which they were intended. As religious men are thought to be good men, deserving of respect and reverence, the reputation of goodness may be sought for itself. The trust and admiration which rightly belong to a holy life, with all the power and influence which they create, may be falsely won, and used for selfish and worldly purposes. The outward forms may even serve as a cloak for a life of secret sin. As Rochefoucauld said, " Hypocrisy is the homage which vice pays to virtue."

But why is hypocrisy, and especially the hypocrisy of the Pharisees, regarded by Jesus as the chief of sins ? Others may seem more hateful and heinous to us, more deserving of watchfulness and warning. Why did He lift up this sin to such bad eminence, and warn His disciples against it " first of all ? " Can we analyse it, and see it in its essential character as He saw it ?

1. It is a form of falsehood, and truth is a fundamental virtue not only of religion but of manhood. Its presence in a character is like a crack in a structure which lessens its strength, or like a flaw in a bell which mars its tone. If there is one sphere where truth is required more than another, it

First of all, Beware of Hypocrisy

is in the interior life. " Behold," it is said, " Thou requirest truth in the inward parts." Falseness there is falseness everywhere. The real man is what he is in the darkness of his secret personal life of thought and desire, where each is free to live according to his liking. But the man as he appears to his fellows may be as different from the inner reality as Dr. Jekyll was from Mr. Hyde. (I suppose Stevenson named him in that way because he *hides* in each of us!) A man may not be a hypocrite who is conscious of an inconsistency between what he is, and what he appears to be. The truest of men have often been burdened by the shame of undeserved praise or reputation. It is a universal wail that while we would do good evil is present with us. Hypocrisy arises when the inconsistency is not regarded as a failure to live up to what we are supposed to be, but as an art in which we take pride, because we have succeeded in passing for what we really are not. There is an imitativeness which is noble and an imitativeness which is ignoble. We may imitate those who are admired, because we love the qualities which they possess, and desire to be like them, or we may imitate them because we wish to gain the admiration which they have deserved, without the virtues which secured it for them. The chameleon changes its colour according to its background, that it may be safe from its enemies. It does so instinctively. The hypocrite adopts the forms of those whom he imitates to secure something which he would not obtain if he sought for it directly. He, too, comes to do it instinctively. The habit of life becomes his nature. So long as the sense of duplicity remains, the nature is smitten with a paralysing weakness. The attainment of strength of character is impossible. The evil or selfish motive destroys the helpful influence which might come from the practice of what is good. The two forces neutralise one another, and result in no virtuous achievement. Gradually the vital power of motive overcomes whatever good influence might arise from the performance of deeds which really belong to a virtuous or religious life. The sense of duplicity is lost. The life becomes a unity, but its unity is evil. Its strength goes out with undivided power through a character which is corrupted. Nobility of life is only possible when the inward aspirations after good, and the outward actions are in harmony. " The goal and the way are one."* " Unity is strength " in this sphere as in all others. The single eye can see, and the undivided heart can attain, what is beyond the vision and power of the hypocrite. He who would reach the heights of character must " First of all, beware of hypocrisy."

* Mazzini.

First of all, Beware of Hypocrisy

2. It is a subtle form of idolatry. The Pharisees practised almsgiving, prayer, and fasting that they might be seen of men. Their religious and charitable observances were not inspired by the desire to please God, but to please men. The reverence and respect which should be given to God alone were transferred to His image. They did not live in the sight of God and think of how they might be accepted of Him; they lived in the sight of men, and all their works were done that they might be seen of them. Man was their God. Yet if we look a little closer at the image which the Pharisees worshipped, we shall see that beyond the world which they sought to please there was the little god " Self," to which the praise of the world was like incense. The sacrifices and service, which were ostentatiously offered to the Most High, were really offered to the world, that the little god " Self " might delight in the admiration and reverence which they called forth. They were not disappointed; they " had their reward." They obtained honour from men by their apparent religiousness. The seemly moralities and holy observances, which belong to the life of faith and true devotion, were prostituted to self-interest and social advantages. The forms and methods which were created by spiritual men for the service of God and the growth of holiness in

the soul were perverted to the glorification of " Self."

Their religion was a masked egotism, a disguised worldliness. Degradation was inevitable. Men instinctively fashion themselves after the likeness of the God whom they worship. He is the ideal of good to them, the perfect embodiment of all that is admirable or desirable. No one can rise higher than his ideal. It is the secret ambitions and aspirations of the soul that lift or degrade us. It is the objects of desire that control our movements, and shape our characters. The ruling passion can subdue all things, even the most sacred things, to itself. It can dare to make the Most Holy, and the service which is His due, its means and methods of obtaining satisfaction for its overmastering cravings. The very means by which self is subdued may be employed for its aggrandisement. Hypocrisy becomes a horror when we realise how it debases to low uses what is intended for man's redemption.

3. The evil of hypocrisy shows itself also in the emphasis which it lays on the externals of religion. These ought to be the expression of an inward devotion ; the exercises by which the soul confesses and strengthens its loyalty towards God. " Spirit and truth " should be their prevailing characteristics. The spirit created them for itself,

First of all, Beware of Hypocrisy

and, apart from its vitalising energy, they are but
lifeless forms, without worth or meaning. To
the spiritually-minded man the forms have no
value in themselves, but the unspiritual and hypo-
critical look upon them as matters of great importance. " Ritualism," as one has said, " is religion
made easy," and that is exactly what they require.
The zealous performance of certain acts, careful
attention to sacred times and seasons, scrupulous
obedience to the letter of the law, become the chief
concern. The observances which give the quickest
and best returns are the most important. Religion
is separated from life, and loses its power of control.
It is identified with ceremonies, sacrifices, services,
not with conscience, conduct and self-sacrifice.
The hypocrite degrades religion by using it for his
own selfish or worldly ends. The more he insists
on the importance of observing its forms, the more
is it debased. He becomes the destroyer of what
he misuses, and takes from men the inspiration
and consolation which the exercises of worship
are fitted to provide. However carefully the
hypocrite may conceal his real character, it is revealed
at some time or other. The veil cannot always be
worn, and those who catch sight of the hidden
hypocrisy often rush to the rash conclusion that
there is no reality in any profession of religion.
They turn away from the Churches in disgust and

anger, and reject with loathing all the recognised forms of worship.   In the reaction of their discovery of falsity in some religious professor, they are carried into opposition to religion itself. Because one man has deceived them, they lose their trust in God. Religious observances become hateful to them, and they will not listen to any appeal which would lead them to a spiritual conception of God and His worship.   Like the clown in *A Midsummer Night's Dream*, they say, " Words are grown so false, that I am loath to reason with them."   They conclude, however unwisely, that if the practice of religious observances can be associated with hypocrisy, it is of no real value in the life of men.   This was one of the ways in which the Pharisees " shut up the Kingdom of Heaven against men."   Their inconsistencies made even true religion hateful. They had taken away the " key of knowledge." Not only did they keep the people in ignorance, but they led them astray. They made religion a yoke " which was intolerable " (Acts xv. 10). " The salt had lost its savour " through their hypocrisy.

4.   But however great is the injury which hypocrites devise for others, the injury which they procure for themselves is vastly greater. The leaven of insincerity works within them, secretly and steadily, until their whole nature is leavened.

First of all, Beware of Hypocrisy

The power of distinguishing between the false and the true is lost ; the pretence is taken for the reality. Deceiving others they at last deceive themselves. Using the forms of religion that they may win the reputation of being religious, they fall into the delusion that they are truly religious men. They come to believe in their lie, and the truth itself seems false to them. Of all states of sin, this is the worst and most hopeless. Barriers have been raised up against repentance. Conscience is silenced by the proofs of zeal and goodness which abound in life. If these do not effectually quiet the inward monitor, additional earnestness in morality and worship is employed to do so. Their vision is blindness, though they call it sight. The delusion becomes so complete that those who disagree with them are by that very fact proved to be in the wrong. Hypocrisy and persecution are as closely related as parent and child. Opposition between Jesus and the Pharisees was inevitable. His truth seemed to them the greatest falsehood : Himself an enemy of righteousness. He appeared to be so far astray in what He taught, that they believed His works of mercy were performed by Beelzebub, the prince of the demons. It was an act of righteous-ness to oppose Him ; they thought that they were doing God service when they crucified Him. The men who hounded the Best to the Cross were convinced of their own rightness and of His wickedness. Good and evil had changed names ; evil was good to them and goodness was evil. So their sin became the sin against the Holy Ghost—that hath never forgiveness, because they had destroyed their power of distinguishing between right and wrong, blinded themselves to their own falsity, and exhausted the possibilities of repentance. The grace and wisdom of Jesus, the holiness of His character, the spiritual wonder of the Kingdom of God, were alien to their minds. They saw no beauty in Him that they should desire Him. The crucifixion of Jesus is the revelation of the evil of hypocrisy. It is the crowning evidence that it is the sin of sins.

5. As we think closely of the subtle, pervasive and destructive power of hypocrisy, we see that it takes its place beside the love of money as " a root of all evil." There is not one of the Ten Commandments which it may not break. It sets up another God for the worship of the soul. It puts God's image in the place which God alone should occupy. It takes His name in vain. It misuses sacred days and seasons. It is ruinous to all the instincts of true reverence. It kills the soul of the hypocrite, and is often instrumental in killing the souls of others, and in taking away also the life of the body. It is an act of spiritual unfaithful-

ness. It is a form of theft; the hypocrite steals the reverence with which his zeal is credited. It is a species of false witness, and it has its source in covetousness.

It is no wonder that our Lord warned His disciples so earnestly against this powerful and prolific sin. We may even say that one of the chief aims which He set before Himself in His ministry was the unmasking of the hypocrite. The thoroughness with which He did the work is evidence of its supreme importance. In the whole range of literature there are no such passages as those which are addressed to the Pharisees in the Gospels. If there is one thing which His disciples were to understand it was the evil of hypocrisy.

6. Not only did He denounce the sin, but He showed how it was to be avoided. The three prominent religious practices in which the Pharisees delighted were—almsgiving, prayer and fasting. It was in connection with these that they, for the most part, found the reward which they sought. Our Lord uses them as illustrations of their sin, and gives the rule by which " His own " would be delivered from it. Charity to the poor is a natural and instinctive virtue of the religious man. The Pharisees practised almsgiving, and did so with such ostentation, that Jesus said it was as if they sounded a trumpet before them. The virtue of charity was

highly valued among them. It was a Rabbinical maxim that "almsgiving was the equivalent of all the virtues." But their acts of charity were inspired by their desire to be seen and praised of men. They were self-seekers, buying the favour of men by their gifts to the poor. Jesus denounced them as hypocrites, and laid down the simple rule for His disciples which would effectually protect them from their sin. It was the publicity of the act which was its snare, therefore He said, " Let not thy left hand know what thy right hand doeth."

Prayer is also universally regarded as an act of religion. It is the " vital breath " of sanctity. The Pharisees prayed, said long prayers, standing at corners, where the people of two streets might see and admire their devotion. They pretended to be communing with God, and, lo ! their eyes were half open that they might mark how many were looking at them. They even timed their movements that the hour of prayer should find them in some public place. Their prayers had no relation to their secret personal needs. They were not praying, but play-acting. They sought not blessing from God, but praise from men. The holiest act and the supremest privilege was prostituted to selfish aims. Again, our Lord gave the saving rule, " Pray to thy Father who seeth in secret."

First of all, Beware of Hypocrisy

Nothing else will serve to save His disciples from this danger. Public prayer is at times a necessity, but men will only be protected from its snares if they keep up the habit of frequent and fervent private prayer.

Fasting also stands among the acts of a religious life. It was much more honoured among the Jews than it is among ourselves. To the Pharisees it proved to be a cheap and simple method of obtaining credit with men. There was no need to fast; all that was necessary was the appearance of fasting. So they disfigured their faces that they might seem unto men to fast. The more they disfigured themselves the more evident was it that they were fasting. Our Lord does not enjoin fasting. He simply assumes that it will be continued as one of the exercises of religious men. But He lays down the injunction which will make fasting a reality, and enable His disciples to escape the danger of the practice. They were to use an innocent form of hypocrisy. They were to anoint their heads and wash their faces, that they might not appear unto men to fast, but " unto their Father who seeth in secret."

One thing appears in every one of these illustrations. The snare of any observance connected with religion lies in its publicity. Wherever there is a possibility of praise from men there is danger of the act of piety being performed for the sake of praise. Jesus seems to lay no stress at all on the observance of forms of religion. His great principle is that they who worship the Father " must worship Him in spirit and in truth." It is possible to do so in the presence of others, or else all meetings for worship in public or in private would be impossible for the Christian. But the act of social worship, if it is to be preserved from dangerous influences, must have behind it the practice of secret devotion. " Thou God seest me " must ever dominate the thoughts of the worshipper.

First Cleanse that which is Within

" Father of Lights, how blind is he
    Who sprinkles the altar he rears to Thee,
    With the blood and tears of humanity."
                                    WHITTIER.

    " In the heart of sin
        Doth Hell begin
    'Tis not below ; 'tis not above
        It lieth within ; it lieth within."
                                    SIDNEY LANIER.

" O cleanse Thou me without, within,
    Or purge with fire, if that must be—
    No matter how, if only sin
        Die out of me."

CHAPTER XII

" FIRST CLEANSE THAT WHICH IS WITHIN "

THE distinction of clean and unclean belongs to a
form of religion which Jesus has destroyed. It is
difficult for us to re-create for ourselves the condition
of mind to which such a matter was of transcendent
importance. It pervaded not only the religious life
of the Jews, but is a characteristic of all ethnic
religions. Its roots lie far back in the dark period
of human life which is beyond the light of history.
It is an artificial distinction, based on ritual or ceremonial considerations, though it is possible that in
some cases it was enforced for sanitary reasons.
Among the Jews " the rules relating to it were
developed to a most painful minuteness. Casuistry
ran riot in this inviting field. . . . The largest
of the six books of the Mishna is devoted to it.
Thirty chapters are given to the single subject of
vessels." *

The Pharisees were specially addicted to the
observance of all such regulations. Not only did

* UNCLEAN. Art. in Hastings' " Dictionary of the Bible."

they make much of washing the hands before eating, but there were " many other things which they received to hold, as the washing of cups and pots, of brazen vessels and tables " (Mark vii. 4). Their devotion was so great that the Sadducees taunted them with the sneer that " they would soon be cleansing the face of the sun ! " Our familiar proverb " Cleanliness is next to godliness " does not express the intensity of their convictions. They would have said that " Cleanliness is godliness." Elaborate forms of purification held a chief place in their idea of religion. Goodness, righteousness, truth and mercy were matters of secondary importance. They cleansed " the outside of the cup and of the platter " but within they were " full of extortion and excess " (Matthew xxiii. 25). Their religious energies were misdirected. They were neglecting the essential things, and substituting for them the veriest trifles. In plain and definite terms Jesus corrected their error. He recognised the importance of cleanliness, but He did not limit it to the outside of things, or regard it as of primary consideration. He would have them cleanse the contents of the cup and platter as well as the vessels themselves. He interprets cleansing spiritually and makes inner purity the supreme duty.

1. The contents of the cup and platter represent all that men may hold as their own, and use for their

First Cleanse that which is Within

support or pleasure. The possession of the good things of this life is not forbidden. A " full cup " is not condemned as an unholy thing. But men must take care that what they have is " clean." The cup and platter of the Pharisees, which were so scrupulously washed, contained what had been wrongfully gained. They were " full of extortion." These holy men were not above the meanness of robbing widows' houses. They were able to live in wealth and provide themselves with dainties from their tyrannous and greedy exactions.* They deluded themselves with the idea that the ceremonial washing of their vessels sanctified all that they contained. Ritual not righteousness was the chief

* " There was a widow who had two orphan daughters. She had a field, and when she wanted to plough it, some one came and said to her, ' Thou shalt not plough with an ox and an ass.' When she wanted to sow, he said, ' Thou shalt not sow with divers kinds of seeds.' When she wanted to reap, he said, ' Thou shalt leave handfuls and a corner for the poor.' When she was preparing her threshing-floor he said, ' Give me the *terumah*, and the first and second tithes.' She met all his demands, and then [not liking all this interference] sold her field and bought two ewes, that she might get clothing from their wool, and some gain from their lambs. When they lambed, came Aaron, and said, ' Give me the first-fruits, for thus saith God to me, " Every firstling that opens the matrix is mine." ' She gave him the two lambs. When the shearing came, he said, ' Give me the first-fruits of the shearing.' She did so, and then said, ' I cannot stand before this man. I will kill my ewes and eat them.' After she had killed them, he came and said, ' Give me the shoulder and the breast.' The woman said, ' Am I not free from this man even after I have killed my ewes ? Lo ! I make these a *Cherem*—consecrated to God.' Then Araon said, ' It is all mine, for God hath said, " Everything devoted in Israel shall be thine." ' So he took it all and departed, and left the widow and her daughters weeping."—Quoted by FARRAR, "Expositor," First Series, vol. v., p. 439.

matter. But Jesus said " Cleanse first that which is within the cup and platter."

As we study this saying in its connection, we see that religion has to do with men's possessions, and especially with the way in which they have been acquired. No amount of religious ceremonial will sanctify what has been secured by injustice or dishonesty. The outward life may be replete with forms of religion, and win from men a reputation for godliness, but Jesus cares for none of these things. He looks to the manner in which men have gained what they possess. He will not accept a man as religious, however saintly he may appear, or regard his wealth as " clean," be it much or little, whose possessions are stained and defiled with extortion. Righteousness is with Him the first consideration.

This is a truth which we need to remember. Religion has a body and a soul, a form and a spirit. It has methods of worship and times and places set apart for their observance. But the soul or spirit is the essential thing. It is confined to no place or time, but pervades the whole of life. It may be strong or weak, but wherever it exists, nothing can be kept apart from its influence. Unhappily, the form may be imitated, and regarded as having a moral value. Men may appear to be religious, who do not live righteously. They may acknowledge

First Cleanse that which is Within

the Lord Jesus in Church and Creed and deny Him in the market-place. Even where there is a sincere devotion to the Saviour, it may be so imperfect or feeble that it fails to overcome the temptations which beset the Christian in the world. The love of money is a passion of such strength, that it can obscure the outlook, confuse the moral issues and weaken the voice of conscience. The complicated arrangements of commercial life, the "sharp" methods of doing business which claim to be legitimate because of long established usage, help to conceal the connection between profit on the one side and loss on the other.

The sin of the Pharisee is with us still. Men take pride in what the Lord Jesus will condemn ; they may be satisfied with what they call " success," when He would name it otherwise. They may deceive themselves with the vain imagination that diligent attendance at public worship, frequent appearances on religious platforms, and the giving of countenance and support to every good cause, absolve them from the imperative necessity of individual righteousness. But the Lord Jesus will scrutinise the methods of business and pass judgment on the results in accordance with His demand for righteousness.

The bitter accusations which are hurled against the Church of Christ to-day, by many of those who have forsaken her, have this as their burden, that men of wealth among her members are honoured with little or no regard to the means by which their money was gained. These complaints are an echo of the teaching of Jesus which the Church has too much forgotten or neglected. He did care much for what men had, for the Gospels are full of His teaching concerning the responsibilities of wealth. But to a far larger degree He emphasised the importance of personal righteousness. All the forms of worship are a mockery without it. They no more affect the man who observes them than the washing of the cup and platter of the Pharisees sanctified what they contained.

We must examine our possessions in the light of Christ. What judgment would He pass upon our prosperity? He will never ask, Is it much or little? but, Is it honest or dishonest? Was any one oppressed or defrauded because of it? We may not see the connection between the fulness of the cup and platter and the extremities to which men and women are sometimes reduced, but in the eyes of " Him with whom we have to do " they may lie together as cause and effect. He " seeth not as man seeth," and our good things may be evil things to Him; our profits losses; our success our condemnation. He neither values the rich for his wealth nor the poor for his poverty. He looks to

First Cleanse that which is Within

the spirit of the life of each ; to the way in which men have come to the one condition or the other. Where religion is a reality it will sanctify the means of gain. Jesus will test it by its influence there. The seemly ceremonies of religious worship are an abomination to Him, if the cup and platter are " full of extortion."

2. The Pharisees were guilty of another error. The contents of the cup and platter were not only gained by extortion, but were used in excess. They fared sumptuously, and imagined that they sanctified " excess " by the ceremonial cleansing of the vessels from which they ate and drank. They put such cleansing in place of a temperate and charitable use of food and drink. But our Lord would have them cleanse their use of food and drink from all excess. There may be sinful abuse as well as a sinful getting, and no amount of ceremonial observance will put it right. Religion is not a mechanical expedient but a spiritual energy. It lays its wise restraint upon appetite. Its forms will never justify excess. Forms of religion did not keep the Pharisees from sin. They professed to eat and drink religiously, but they were gluttons and winebibbers all the same. They were right in their principle, but wrong in the method of carrying it out. Religion has to do with eating and drinking. Our Lord would make the principle a vital reality, a controlling power and not

a futile observance.   The Pauline rule that we should
" eat and drink to the glory of God," was derived
from His teaching.   In my boyhood I remember
hearing of an old man who used to " say grace "
before drinking a glass of whisky.   Men smiled as
they told the story, but why should they have
smiled ?   If his " saying grace " was a truly
religious act, was he not carrying out the Pauline
principle ?   If his example could be followed in
spirit and truth would there not be a lessening, if
not an end, of our national sin ?   Would there be
excess in anything, if everything was used with a
consciousness of God's presence and goodness, and
a sincere desire for His glory ?   The " saying
grace," however, may be as formal and as useless
as the washing of cups and platters.   It must be a
spiritual exercise if it is to help us to eat our meat
" with gladness and singleness of heart, praising
God."

3. But the contents of the cup and platter
stand for more than meat and drink.   " Excess "
may be practised in many other forms than in eating
and drinking.   We may spend our means waste-
fully, selfishly, luxuriously, in dress, amusements,
and the conduct of our personal and household
affairs.   An Indian missionary, when at home on
furlough, after a long absence from this country,
once said to me that what struck him most was the

First Cleanse that which is Within

vast increase in the luxuries of life. This witness
is true. On every side the increase is visible. Not
only in the world of fashion, but also in what may
be called Christian society, this fact is manifest.
Christ is not the foe of comfort, beauty or pleasure.
He has not taught us that God is honoured by
ugliness, sordidness, or gloom. God can be honoured
in comfort and by beauty as well as in poverty and
mean attire. It is the spirit of the life which He
regards. If men and women are His children, they
will make His glory the end and rule of all expend-
iture. Their use of what they have will be a matter
and a method of religion. If this were done, the
poor and needy would be better cared for, and the
work of Christ at home and abroad would not tarry
for lack of means.

4. In the corresponding passage in the Gospel
according to St. Luke (xi. 41, R.V.), our Lord said
" Howbeit, give for alms those things which are
within, and behold all things are clean unto you."
It is not consistent with the general teaching of
Jesus to interpret this saying as if the giving of
alms, even to the extent of giving everything, could
atone for extortion and excess in the amassing or
using of wealth. Our Lord speaks not of atonement,
but of cleansing. Gifts to the poor have as little
influence in that direction as the washing of cup and
platter. They may even lead to more persistent

sin in money getting, if it is understood that they can sanctify dishonest gains. But it is consistent with His teaching to interpret the saying as laying down the principle that love—which is the only inspiration of true charity—will cleanse everything. If love prompts the giving it will also control the getting. A wise and tender consideration for others, which is the foundation of all real charity, will effectually check all methods and forms of extortion, injustice and dishonesty. It is in this way that the strange saying of our Lord is to be understood. There is no antidote for the poison of avarice but love.

5. But the rebuke of the Saviour goes far beyond these matters of getting and spending. In this figurative way He deals with the inner and outer life of man. The Pharisees laid stress on the outward life, on forms of religion which men could see. Our Lord lays stress on the condition of the heart, on the religion of spirit and truth which only God could see. Jesus had no quarrel with the forms of religious profession. He went to the synagogues and the Temple to worship. He taught men to pray in social prayer. He instituted the two great rites of the Christian Church—Baptism and the Lord's Supper. But forms of religion are secondary matters to Him. They are only of value as expressions and aids of devotion. It is not the outer gilding but the gold that He desires. Forms of worship have no

First Cleanse that which is Within

meaning except as they help to express and increase an inward devotion. Religion can only really influence the life when it first rules in the heart. If the heart is clean, the life will be clean also. If the spirit is religious, the deeds and words will be of the same character. The flower and fruit are but the ripening and manifestation of the hidden sap that flows in the branches and the stem. The constant danger is that men should be content with appearances of goodness. It is so much easier to have the form of godliness than to have the power of it. Many influences are at work upon us, inducing us to give attention to the outward expressions of devotion, but nothing except a pure desire to please God will lead us to cultivate that inward purity, which is of greater worth in His sight than all temples, creeds, or ceremonies.

Therefore we must cleanse first the interior life, that the exterior may be clean also. The springs of thought and desire must be purified from all insincerity and unholiness, that word and deed may flow forth in purity and truth. If we live as in the presence of God, we shall be truly holy in the sight of men. They who know anything of the joy of winning His approval will never be tempted to seek, instead of it, the favour or applause of men.

6. The last sentence was pronounced against the outward carefulness of the Pharisees, when our Lord

explained His parable about real defilement, " Do ye not perceive that whatever thing from without entereth into the man, it cannot defile him, because it entereth not into his heart, but into the belly and goeth out into the draught ? " (Mark vii. 18, 19). The significance of this utterance was not seen when it was spoken. It dawned upon the disciples at a later time, and then the note was added by some teacher or editor in the Apostolic age, indicating that by saying this, He was " purging all meats." The conservative spirit of the Jewish Christians maintained the distinction between clean and unclean for a time, but it gradually disappeared from the thought and practice of the Church. We see evidence of its continuance after the death of Jesus, in the answer of St. Peter to the words of the angel as he was bidden kill and eat of the clean and unclean beasts and birds that appeared to be let down from heaven in a great sheet. He said, " Not so, Lord, for I have never eaten anything that is common or unclean." It may have been the vision which recalled to him the parable of the Master, and led him to interpret it in the way that is recorded in Mark. But the words of the Lord Jesus created a revolution in religious thought and life. Following His guidance, His disciples have been freed from the yoke of bondage which the distinction laid upon the Jews ; they have been delivered from the snare which lay

First Cleanse that which is Within

in the association of evil with what is material, and they have been led to look within for the defiling influences which marred their holiest aspirations, and brought them under the power of temptation. Christ's emphasis on the inwardness of sin was really an act of redemption. Many consequences have flowed from it. Religion has become both a higher and deeper experience. The strife with sin has become more acute and painful. The need and difficulty of cleansing the heart are greater than ever were the need and difficulty of an outward cleansing. But those who have accepted the word of Jesus know that He who revealed the defilement of the heart as the one source of sin also opened a fountain for sin and for uncleanness. The ancient but constant prayer of the spiritually minded man, " Create in me a clean heart, O God," has had its answer in Him.

First Cast Out the Beam

" It was my custom in youth," said a celebrated
Persian writer, " to rise from my sleep, to watch and
pray and read the Koran. One night when thus
engaged, my father, who was a man of practical
virtue, awoke. ' Behold,' I said, ' thine other children are lost in irreligious slumber, while I alone
awake and praise God.' ' Son of my soul,' he said,
' It were better for thee to be lost in irreligious
slumber, than to awake and despise thy brethren.' "

" Human nature suffers from a passion to be
instructive."—Mrs. H. Bland.

    " ' Where have you been, my brother ?
       For I missed you from the street.'
   ' I have been away for a night and a day
      On the Lord God's judgment seat.'

   ' And what did you see, my brother,
      When your judging there was done ? '
   ' Weeds in my garden, dust in my door,
      And my flowers all dead in the sun.

   ' And the lesson I brought with me,
      Like silence from above—
  On God's judgment throne, there is room alone
      For Him whose heart is love.' "

CHAPTER XIII

" FIRST CAST OUT THE BEAM "

WE are startled by the emphatic prohibition of judgment with which the last section (Matthew vii.) of the Sermon on the Mount begins. In every decision we make, in every opinion we form, judgment enters as a necessary and inevitable element. It is part of the discipline of life, from which there is no escape. How then can we obey the command " Judge not " ?

But we must see to it that we have rightly understood the words of Jesus. He Himself exercised judgment. The word " hypocrite " which is found in this passage is a word of judgment. When He bids us " Beware of men," or asks " Why do ye not of your own selves judge what is right ? " He is authorising judgment. Our difficulty springs from a common source. We take a single precept by itself, and seek to understand it apart from its context, with the result that we confuse ourselves, and miss the Master's meaning. We must read the whole context if we would understand any part of it. When

The First Things of Jesus

we do so we see that it is unthinking, unsympathetic, self-righteous judgments which He forbids ; moral criticisms by those who are not qualified to act as censors of faults or sins from which they themselves are not free.

We can even say that He explicitly leaves room for judgment when He says, " Then shalt thou see clearly to cast out the mote that is in thy brother's eye." The brother with a mote in his eye is greatly in need of assistance, but we must recognise that the mote is there before we can offer to remove it. " Helping lame dogs over stiles " is a proverbial description of a gracious kindness. It involves, however, the judgment that the dogs are lame ! To read the words of Jesus as if they forbade all judgment would make it impossible to obey the Golden Rule, or yield to the impulses of the kindly Christian spirit which prompts us to help wherever the need of help is seen.

We *have* a duty to discharge in relation to the mote that is in our brother's eye, but we must see to it that our duty in regard to the beam in our eye— if it is there—is attended to first. The Pharisaic type of mind, which is blinded by prejudice and bound by petty rules, is incapable of the delicate task of judgment. It is in reference to it that Jesus speaks these graphic words of prohibition and warning.

First Cast Out the Beam

1. " First cast out the beam out of thine own eye " (Matthew vii. 5) is evidently a proverb of the carpenter's workshop, and may have come to the knowledge of Jesus when He was working with Joseph in Nazareth. It is a Jewish proverb ; but the fault at which it strikes is one of human nature. Men and women are prone to judge other people without having first judged themselves. The sins and faults which others show bulk more largely in their minds than those which belong to themselves.

The fable of the man who carried two wallets has a wide application. He carried one on his breast, which was so full and heavy that it bowed him down. He carried the other on his back, but it was so light and empty that he was scarcely conscious of its weight. The wallet on the breast was stuffed with the sins of his neighbours ; the wallet on the back contained his own few faults ! We smile at the fable, but we dare not smile at the truth which it teaches.

Most of us are remarkably blind to our own inconsistencies. Sometimes the lack of perception is shown in an amusing way. Two young girl companions were warmly attached to each other. One of them in the rash enthusiasm of friendship proposed, as a means of mutual improvement, that they should each tell the faults which they saw in one another.   She urged her friend to begin.   After much persuasion she yielded, and, in the most delicate manner possible, hinted that her friend was lacking in the grace of charity in her judgments. The result was surprising.   The girl who had invited the criticism denied the charge indignantly—" Whatever fault she had it was not that."   Alas, the friendship was broken !   The test was too severe, for,

> " Many will beseech their friends
> To tell them of their faults, which being told
> Will ne'er forgive the tellers."*

The men and women who suffer from colour-blindness are few, compared with those who do not see their own shortcomings.   The proud rarely know that they are proud ; the obstinate that they are obstinate ;   the selfish that they are selfish. There is an unconsciousness of fault as well as an unconsciousness of virtue.   Not to know one's own goodness is an additional grace, not to know our own failings is an additional failing.

It was said of the late Mr. Matthew Arnold that " he had the power of seeing his own faults (in others) without recognising that they were his own " !   He could say plain and piercing words about them, all unconscious that his friends applied them to himself. It is a remarkably common failing.   The intolerant

* "Philip van Artevelde."

First Cast Out the Beam

are heard denouncing intolerance ; the niggardly
say most in scorn of what they think niggardly.

Some are eager to correct the faults of others
without a single thought that they may need correction themselves. The author of that interesting
book, " How to be Happy though Married," says
that a copy of it came into the hands of a married
lady, who put paper marks in the pages which deal
with the duties of husbands to wives, and laid it
in her husband's way, in the hope that he would
profit by the advice. He found the book, and read
the pages which were marked, but when he turned
to the chapter which is addressed to wives he discovered that the leaves were uncut !

A member of a church once complained to her
minister that she had been twenty-five years in the
church and no one had spoken to her. " What ! "
said he, " Do you mean to tell me that you have been
twenty-five years in this church and you have spoken
to nobody ? " Complaints of stiffness and coldness
in churches are not uncommon, but as a rule it is
the stiff and cold who make complaints. We can
imagine an iceberg complaining of the chilliness of
the atmosphere which surrounds it, and forgetting
that an iceberg radiates cold, as a fire radiates heat.

In disputes and controversies it is a common failing to overlook the weak points in our own arguments
and the strong points in the arguments of our oppo-

nents. We are scornful of the statements which they advance, and find a joy in detailing the absurdities and inconsistencies which are involved in their position.

The more zealous we are in advancing our own opinions, the more we are annoyed by the zeal of those who differ from us. We profess to be animated by the love of truth, while it is nothing but stubborn self-will and pride, such as we charge against our opponent, which is the source of our zeal. Fanaticism and bigotry are the offspring of this blindness, and all the bitterness of our disputes comes from it.

The rebuke which Cromwell addressed to the Presbyterian ministers is one which should be kept in mind by all who engage in controversy—" I beseech you, my brethren, by the mercies of God, to think it possible that you may be mistaken." All the truth is not generally on one side, but the beam in our own eye prevents us from recognising this simple and elementary fact.

2. The blindness to the fault in ourselves which we condemn in others is so universal, that we should ask if the power to see a fault in another is not the sign that that very fault is in ourselves. May it not be that the " mote " is the shadow of the " beam " ; that it is the evil in our own hearts which opens our eyes to recognise it elsewhere ?

First Cast Out the Beam

In that terrible story, "The Scarlet Letter," it is said of Hester the woman who bore the mark of sin, "that, walking to and fro with those lonely footsteps in the little world with which she was outwardly connected, it now and then appeared to her as if the scarlet letter had endowed her with a new sense. She shuddered to believe, and yet could not help believing, that it gave her a sympathetic knowledge of hidden sin in the hearts of others. She was terror-stricken by the revelations which were thus made." Was it not rather the sin which she had done, and not the letter which she wore as a punishment, that gave her that dread insight?

Is not Tennyson's searching phrase deeply significant, "Every man imputes himself"? The sin we suspect is the sin that we ourselves know; the motive we impute is the motive whose power we recognise. We find our own complexion everywhere. Our eyes are opened. An innocent child sees nothing but colour, movement and stories in pictures, scenes and books which are stained and permeated with the leprosy of uncleanness to the man whose innocency is a long lost and forgotten shield. It seems as if the experience of sin had often the strange power of revealing and concealing —making us aware of it in others, while it blinds us to its presence in ourselves.

The First Things of Jesus

It is not the man of true charity who accuses others of uncharitableness, for " he thinketh no evil, and hopeth all things." It is the uncharitable who are the accusers of the brethren in this matter. " Generally speaking, it is true that people who are easily bored are bores themselves—and go through life rejoicing, and convinced that their conversation is a blessing, and their advice a treasure to those who get it."*

Rochefoucauld laid his unerring finger on a failing of humanity when he said, " It is our own vanity which makes the vanity of others intolerable." May it not be because of this deep principle in the life of man that it is said, " With what measure ye mete, it shall be measured to you again " ? It is our own sin that we see, and the judgment we give is the judgment we deserve.

3. Nay, more, so blind and foolish are we, that we can act the part of censor when the faults which we condemn are smaller than our own. We complain of the " mote," and do not see " the beam." The sensitive plant might be imagined as complaining of the insensibility of other plants to its sufferings, while it remains unmoved when the giant oak falls close beside it. What a fuss we make over our little griefs and troubles ! How unkind others seem because they do not sympathise with us as we expect !

* F. M. Crawford, " Marion Darche."

First Cast Out the Beam

There is no more common complaint than the lack of appreciation. Its presence "puts light and colour into the greyest lives, and makes them richer." We long for it, and feel as if the sky had lost its brightness, and the world were cold, when it is denied us. Yet the failure to appreciate what others do is much more common, and those who have least claim to it are often most regardless of excellence in others, and are most loud in the complaint that they themselves are not appreciated. Our Lord is revealing a universal fault, and the way to correct it, when He says, " First cast out the beam out of thine own eye."

4. We see something more of the significance of this precept when we recognise that our Lord traces the evil of censorious judgment to hypocrisy. " Thou hypocrite ! " is His judgment on the self-righteous meddler. He pretends to be better than he is. He enjoys a certain sense of satisfaction, a moral superiority, in condemning the sins and faults of others. He sets himself upon a pedestal of virtue to which he has no right. The more scathing the judgment, the more highly he thinks of himself, and the better the reputation he wins from those who do not know him.

But the condemnation of the sins of others is a poor substitute for personal goodness. We never raise ourselves by casting others down ; never make ourselves good by showing that others are bad. The pleasure and reputation of virtue are too easily won. The reality is a treasure for which a great price has to be paid. The pains of self-knowledge, the sorrows of penitence, the humbling of the heart before God, the strain of a life-long effort after new obedience, cost much, and by these alone can true goodness be gained.

Plucking out the mote without having first cast out the beam is seen to be hypocrisy in yet another way. If we are really anxious to have any evil corrected, we shall naturally begin where we have the greatest influence and the greatest interest in its removal.

The man who stands forth as a temperance reformer and condemns the sin of drunkenness is expected first to free himself from all connection with strong drink. The merchant who takes up a prominent position in regard to commercial dishonesty must first cleanse his own business from everything that is shady or unsound. The advocate of peace and arbitration is expected to show his devotion to these lofty principles by his readiness to submit all the disputes in which he is interested to arbitration, and by following assiduously in his own life the things which make for peace.

All other methods of action in such matters are pervaded by insincerity, and tainted by hypocrisy.

First Cast Out the Beam

We can only effectively take part in movements of this kind when we have " first cast out the beam out of our own eye."   And if it is so in the larger proposals of reform, it is all the more essential that the same method should be followed in the more difficult and delicate endeavour to correct a failing or sin in the life of an individual.

The self-righteous meddler is also a hypocrite because he pretends to have the power of helping, when he is entirely destitute of it.   He is a moral quack.   To remove a mote from the eye is a delicate operation.   It demands a clear eye and a steady hand.   The man who has a " beam," or even a " mote," in his own eye is absolutely incapacitated for it.   He is the last person in the world who should attempt it.   He will most likely increase the injury, drive the mote in further instead of taking it out.

5. But the delicacy of removing a mote from the eye is not to be compared with the fineness of touch and the tenderness of action which are required in all attempts at moral correction.   Most men with a fault or sin are unwilling to own that they have it. Even truly Christian men and women show signs of indignation at the first indications of reproof.   They have generally to be convinced that the fault or sin is in them, but who will convince them ?   They will readily own that they are sinners, but to own that

they are guilty of some particular sin is a different matter.   Well may we cry, " Who is sufficient for these things ? "

It is those who are the least qualified for the work of correction who are the most ready to attempt it, and when they do they are surprised that their reproof becomes a boomerang, which hits the " beam " in their own eyes ; and they are forcibly, if not politely, reminded of the proverb, " Physician, heal thyself." Those who are most fully qualified, because they have knowledge of their own hearts, and have sought most earnestly to rid themselves of the faults and sins of which they are conscious, are the most tender in the judgments they make. They are never officious in their offers of assistance. They know too well the vast possibilities of error and of injury, that lie in rash and ignorant dealings with the souls of men. They are too deeply conscious of their own faults and failings to think of passing a censorious judgment on another.

And in humility and love they seek to win the confidence of those whom they would help. In brotherliness, and as fellow-sinners, by prayer, sympathy, love and patience, they endeavour to guide them closer to the Light, where all sin will be revealed, and by whose influence alone it can be removed. They are not indifferent to the sins of their fellows, but, knowing how difficult correction

First Cast Out the Beam

is, they seek rather to let them see Christ that in His light they may see themselves.

The true saints of God are ever the most gentle and hopeful in their criticism of life and act in others. Their severity is for themselves ; their charity is for others. They are more concerned about the beam than about the mote. The great Apostle Paul called himself the chief of sinners. Francis of Assisi wept so much for his sins that he injured his eyesight. Of Erskine of Linlathen it was said, " all who conversed with him in his last years were struck by his ever-deepening sense of sin, and the personal way in which he took this home to himself."

When the " beam " is removed, and we see clearly, we first recognise how much is wrong with ourselves. We are more ready to ask how much we may have done directly or indirectly to cause our brother to offend, than openly to correct him. We recognise that we can only have the true and helpful influence in the deliverance of others in proportion as our own is accomplished. We begin to understand why it is said that " God sent not His Son to condemn the world, but that the world through Him might be saved." Condemnation and saving cannot work together. Love alone can help.

First be Reconciled to thy Brother

"At every little trivial scorn to take offence,
That always shows great pride or little sense."
POPE, *Essay on Criticism*.

"O brother man, fold to thy heart thy brother;
Where pity dwells the peace of God is there;
To worship rightly is to love each other,
Each smile a hymn, each kindly deed a prayer."
WHITTIER.

CHAPTER XIV

" FIRST BE RECONCILED TO THY BROTHER "

WHAT place should worship have in thought and life ? It is the service and joy of Heaven, and should claim the highest place in the activities of earth. When we give the old answer to the question, " What is man's chief end ? "—" To glorify God and enjoy Him for ever," we are using familiar words to express the idea that man has been created for the praise of God. Perhaps the noblest thought of man is that he is a creature who worships, and of the earth, that it is " a place where prayer is wont to be made." With lofty eloquence Martineau has described the universal act of the twilight hours of morning and' evening. " All round the earth on the bordering circle between the darkness and the day a zone of worshippers has ever been spread, looking forth towards the Almighty Tenant of space, one half toward the East, brilliant with dawn, the other to the night descending on the West. The veil of shadow as it shifts has glanced upon adoring souls, and by its touch has cast down a fresh multitude to kneel."

The First Things of Jesus

As we realise the meaning and importance of the act of worship we feel that for men and women the first commandment must ever be " Thou shalt worship the Lord thy God, and Him only shalt thou serve." It expresses the essential relation in which they must stand to Him with whom they have to do. Our Lord, however, seems to set another duty before it, and a duty which at first sight appears to be subordinate to it. He pictures a worshipper standing in the Court of the Temple, waiting for an opportunity of presenting his offering or sacrifice to the priest. While he waits before the altar, the memory of some wrong that he has done comes to his mind. He remembers what " a brother has against him." In such a case, Jesus bids the worshipper leave his gift before the altar, go away instantly, first be reconciled to his brother, and then come and offer his gift.

1. Why does Jesus give this instruction— so emphatically and particularly expressed—a prior place to the first of the Ten Commandments ? How are we to reconcile these apparently conflicting duties ? In the one case it is man's chief end to worship God ; in the other it is his first duty to be reconciled to his brother.

Our Lord is really giving a lesson in worship. He is interpreting the first commandment, " Thou shalt worship the Lord thy God " in the same way

First be Reconciled to thy Brother

as He interpreted the sixth and seventh (Matt. v. 21-32). Just as He showed that these commandments penetrated to the spheres of feeling and desire, and could be broken by angry or lustful emotions, so the first commandment embraced within it the condition of the spirit of the worshipper, and could not be obeyed if wrongful thoughts were cherished, or hurtful deeds were done without repentance. One necessary element in a truly worshipful spirit is kindliness or peace towards man. Reconciliation with man is an essential requirement or preparation for the worship of God. He who has wronged a brother, and persists in the wrong, is not in a right condition to draw near to the Most High. The priest may receive his gift and lay it on the altar, but God does not accept it. Instead of honouring God, such a worshipper is dishonouring Him ; instead of securing the blessing of acceptance, he is bringing upon himself the sentence of rejection.

There is no originality in the principle which is emphasised here. It is found in the old-world story of Cain and Abel. Because Cain was wroth with his brother, the Lord had not respect unto his offering. In that first recorded act of worship, the truth was revealed which Jesus enunciates in the words, " First be reconciled to thy brother, and then come and offer thy gift." It was not the character of the sacrifices which led to the rejection of Cain and the acceptance of Abel. It was the spirit of these primitive worshippers, and especially their feelings towards each other, which God regarded. Our gifts and modes of worship differ greatly from those of Cain and Abel, and from those also to which our Lord referred, but the principle is the same. In our offerings of praise and prayer and money, acceptance or rejection depends upon the condition of our hearts towards those with whom we are related in the bonds of social brotherhood. We must be at peace with our " brother " before we can hope to be accepted of God. It is first the " brother " and then the " Father."

The same lesson is repeated in the petition which our Lord put upon our lips when He taught us to pray, " Forgive us our debts as we forgive our debtors," and when He said, " If ye forgive men their trespasses, your Heavenly Father will also forgive you ; but if ye will not forgive men their trespasses, neither will your Heavenly Father forgive your trespasses " (Matt. vi. 14, 15). The withholding of pardon from a brother becomes something that he has against us, and stands as an obstacle to the forgiveness of God. In both illustrations, our Lord is emphasising the duty of thinking more of what others have against us than of what we may have against them. Injuries which we receive are always apt to seem of greater moment than those which we inflict. We lay greater stress upon our " wrongs " than upon the " wrongs " of others. If we judged them rightly the balance might be against us. But even if it were in our favour, our own exceeding need of the grace and mercy of God demands from us in our approach to Him a spirit of unlimited forgiveness. When we ask God to pardon what He has against us, we must be ready to show a like grace to those by whom we have been offended. Reconciliation with man is an absolute condition of reconciliation with God.

2. In insisting so strongly on this principle our Lord is affirming that God is love and that worship is spiritual. The strife and wrong-doing of men are displeasing to Him. The atmosphere in which He lives is that of love, and nothing unloving can come before Him. He cares most that men should love each other. We must be in harmony with Him if any communication is to pass from us to Him or from Him to us. The instruments employed in wireless telegraphy can only act when they are tuned to the same note. The note of communion between Heaven and earth is love.

The forms of worship, however necessary they may be, are not the chief matter. " The sacrifices of God are a broken spirit ; a broken and a contrite heart, O God, Thou wilt not despise." It is indeed a "broken spirit" which can approach a brother with confession of wrong-doing. Pride, self-righteousness, and impenitence can never exist where such confession is made. The confession to man becomes the proof of the truth of the confession to God. However difficult it may be, God requires it ; but it will bring a blessing which far exceeds its pain. The truth of this spiritual experience can be put to the proof. We know that when we are hard and unforgiving the heavens are as brass above us. Our anger against a brother shuts us out from the loving presence of God. Our prayers sound hollow and unreal, and answer there is none. We lose Him in whose favour is life, whose lovingkindness is better than life. This has been the experience of all who have cherished the unforgiving spirit which shrinks from the way that Christ points out. But those who have sought in faith and humility to exercise the grace of pardon, who have been ready not only to own an injury which they have done, but to forgive an injury which they have received, have found themselves enriched with the blessings of peace and joy. The burdens have been taken from their hearts, the dulness from their spirits ; the light of the face of God has shone on them. The forms of worship which had been only forms become the means of true intercourse with God. They worship God in spirit and in truth who seek first to be reconciled to their brother.

3. This great spiritual duty of reconciliation before worship is not to be held as if men were to be indifferent to the wrongs which they may receive. Christianity takes the anxiety and care for such things out of our hands. It reveals God as the Avenger of the wronged. It bids us "give place unto wrath": that is, to His wrath. He undertakes for those who suffer injuries. "He is the Father of the fatherless, the Judge of the widow, the Shield of the stranger and the Stay of the orphan." "I will repay, saith the Lord."

The man who wrongs another and yet seeks to worship God may hear as the reason why his prayers and offerings are not accepted: " Inasmuch as ye have done it unto one of the least of these ye have done it unto Me." God would guard us from hurting one another by identifying Himself with those whom we would wrong !

4. Further, worship is not an act which is external to the life and feelings of men. There is a unity in one's personality which cannot be broken. What men are as they live among men, they also are when they came before God. The wrong-doer in the world is still a wrong-doer when he seeks to worship God. Religion and life may be separated in thought, but they cannot be separated in reality.

The First Things of Jesus

Men do not leave their sins behind them when they come to pray. The sin is with them even then, for it is in them. The unforgiven grudge, the unconfessed wrong, are brought with the worshipper to the All-Holy and All-Seeing Presence. They rise like the great mountains between us and Him. We cannot be satisfied with the goodness of His house unless God is satisfied with us. Sometimes men and women complain that the services which they once enjoyed are no longer helpful or pleasant ; that they are a weariness to them. They begin to think that the preacher is dull, that the prayers are lifeless, that the singing is poor. It may be true. But there is another possibility. Those who complain may not be prepared for worship. They may bring to the house of God the memory of an injury which has not been confessed, or of a wrong which has not been forgiven. There may be a brother who has something against them. The life outside the Church influences the life within it. Unkind words spoken in selfish anger, advantage taken of the weak or helpless, tyrannous disregard of the feelings of others— how seldom do people think that it is these things which cause the lack of interest and pleasure which they experience in God's worship! To these Jesus would say, " First be reconciled to thy brother, and then come and offer thy gift " ; then find anew the blessedness of prayer, and rejoice once more in the presence of God ; then make melody in the heart which could not sing before.

What is said of individuals is also to be said of Churches. As we think of the divisions of Christendom, and above all of the strife and enmities which exist between different Christian societies, this word becomes an ecclesiastical duty of the most urgent character. Can worship be acceptable where there are revilings, contempt, bitter accusations, uncharitable judgments ? The Church divisions of England and Scotland are enough to explain the absence of power which all the Churches confess with grief. The blessing of God cannot come where there is a breach in the unity of the Spirit. Unity of organisation is not necessary. There may be differences of administration and differences of operation, but unity of faith and spirit, loving recognition of devotion to the same Lord, are absolutely essential. Power will come with peace, and peace with love. " First be reconciled to thy brother " is the secret of revival and expansion.

5. What a touch of truth it is that while the worshipper stands before the altar, the memory of a wrong that he has done comes up in his memory ! The worshipper had some elements of a truly religious life, or he would not have been troubled then. It is when we are really in the presence of God that

the conscience becomes most active, and forgotten sins come to the mind.   It may be taken as a sure sign of spiritual life when we remember our sins as we pray.   Isaiah, when he saw the vision of God in the Temple, and heard the " Holy, Holy, Holy," of the Cherubim, was forced to cry, " Woe is me, for I am undone, for I am a man of unclean lips."   St. Peter, at the revelation of the divine power of Jesus, fell at His feet, and cried, " Depart from me, for I am a sinful man, O Lord."   Spiritual life is proved to be sincere when deep convictions of sin come to us while we pray.   Conscience is quickened as we kneel in God's presence.   In the light of His countenance we see what was hidden from us.   The hour of prayer is the time of self-revealing.   Only let us attend to the convictions of sin which are wrought in us then, and we shall be led through penitence and confession to the pardon and peace of the Face of God.

6. If we are in earnest in our desire to please God, we shall never shrink from the painful and humbling way that takes us to the brother we have wronged. It requires a true and strong religious spirit to carry us thither.   The innate pride of our hearts protests against the humiliation.   A thousand reasons spring up to reinforce it.   We say, " They deserved what was done," or " They should not have opposed me," or " They should have taken better care of their

First be Reconciled to thy Brother

own interests." We dread above all the triumph with which we expect them to exult over us. We shrink from the taunts with which we imagine our confession will be received. We may even say, " They will not listen to us or believe us." It *is* hard to win a brother who has been wronged. But all the while in our inmost hearts we know that we have done wrong, and that even if there had been some provocation the act of wrong was ours. Our deed has to be confessed, though others have had a share in it, and if we are really penitent we shall not be very anxious to apportion the blame. But the dread of meeting with a rebuff is for the most part utterly baseless. It is the creation of our pride and our fears.

In some cases it may happen that confession of wrong is received with scorn, for it takes a truly Christian spirit to receive a confession rightly as well as to make it. But in such a case we have the consolation of knowing that we have obeyed the command of the Lord Jesus, who will reward us with a sense of peace which is worth (and more than worth) the evil experience of a scorned confession. In general, however, our reception will surprise us by its sympathy and kindness. It will certainly be so in the case of any Christian brother who has been wronged by us. We may find that we do not need to say anything.

Our presence, our very look, will be enough to unlock to us our brother's heart. As the prodigal was not allowed to say to his father all that he intended, so will it be with us. The words of forgiveness will scarcely need to be spoken in the joy of finding again the brother who had been lost. Not seldom are the wrongs which the presence of God brings to our memory done to those who love us and whom we love. Sometimes it is the husband who has wounded the wife, or the wife that has vexed the husband. It is brothers who injure brothers, and friends who give pain to friends. They are as troubled as we are by the act of wrong. They will welcome our repentance as the father welcomed the prodigal, but we must take the first step, and, it may be, say the first word. Confession is our duty ; forgiveness is theirs. Let us try the method of the Master. He who knew the heart of man laid down no impossible or futile rule when He said, " First be reconciled to thy brother."

7. There is a note of urgency in the command. Some would read it, " Go away first ; be reconciled to thy brother." With the memory of a wrong stirring in our memories we are to go away at once. We are not to stay till worship is over. The memory of the wrong has come late, but, coming then, worship itself must be postponed till reconciliation is accomplished. The wrong should have been felt and

First be Reconciled to thy Brother

confessed before. Delay has increased the difficulty
of the duty. The gift is to be left beside the altar.
People may remark and wonder, but the man who
would worship God acceptably is not to be deterred
from doing this urgent duty because of what others
may think or say. Better that men should look
and wonder than that God should hide His face
from us. Their criticisms are but the added penalty
which we have brought upon ourselves by
delay.

The Lord Jesus does not mean that it is only at
worship that we remember our sins. His thought
is that if we have not made confession before, we
should be instant in doing our duty then. The
acceptability of the act of worship depends upon
it. If we have delayed so long let us delay no
longer.

> " The penitence is best to bear
> That follows soonest on the sin,
> And guilt's a game where losers fare
> Better than those that seem to win."*

We cannot repent too soon. A late repentance is
better than none, but it may lose the grace of fresh-
ness and freeness. It may have allowed the wrong
to work out bitterness in a brother's soul. Forgiveness is not easy when the offence is old. A quick
repentance meets with a speedy and gracious

* Coventry Patmore.

pardon. The severance which the wrong created has not had time to harden into permanence. The wounded spirit has not had opportunity to brood over its hurt. Reconciliation is easy when it is speedy. Therefore " agree with thine adversary quickly, while thou art in the way with him."

The First Stone

" The sin that you do by two and two
You must pay for one by one."
RUDYARD KIPLING.

" Thou who so lightly dealest death to me,
Be thou then very sure of thine own soul."
STEPHEN NICHOLLS, *The Sin of David*.

" Why should man, who is so strong, always get
the best of it ; and woman, who is so weak, get the
worst, and be forgiven so little ? "
MRS. W. K. CLIFFORD, *A Modern Correspondence*.

" It is not the man without sin who is eager to
cast the first stone, it is always he who can be easily
convicted by his own conscience."
BASIL KING, *The Steps of Honour*.

" This is His divinity,
This His universal plea,
Here is One that loveth thee."

" Then I knew
That I was saved. I never met
His face before, but at first view
I felt quite sure that God had set
Himself to Satan."
R. BROWNING, *Count Gismond*.

CHAPTER XV

"THE FIRST STONE"

"HE that is without sin among you, let him cast the first stone." The story in which these words occur is found only in the Gospel according to St. John (viii. 3-11). Its authenticity is gravely questioned. If we relied on manuscript evidence alone, we should be compelled to admit that it did not form part of the Gospel as it left the hands of the Evangelist. But when we consider its character, and the spirit of its teaching, we feel that it is the record of a real incident in the life of Jesus. No one but Jesus could have acted and spoken as He acts and speaks here. The story is one that could not be invented. Besides, its omission from some of the early manuscripts of this Gospel is easily accounted for. In the early Church it was regarded as a dangerous story—an incident which might be misunderstood. It was thought that too much leniency was shown to the sinful woman, and that it had a tendency to weaken the sacredness of the marriage vow. But whether the narrative formed part of the original Gospel of St. John or not, it bears upon its surface the plain impress of the mind and spirit of Jesus, and we have no doubt as to its truth.

1. When Jesus said, " He that is without sin among you, let him cast the first stone," He was defending Himself against an attack of the Scribes and Pharisees. They were " tempting Him that they might accuse Him." As He was teaching in the Temple, they brought before Him a woman who had been " taken in adultery, in the very act." They set her in the midst of the company which surrounded Jesus, and said, " Moses in the Law commanded us that such should be stoned : but what sayest Thou ? " They had felt the keenness and strength of His condemnation of the forms of " righteousness " in which they took pride. His influence with the people was steadily increasing ; it might reach such a height that their own authority would be destroyed. Something must be done to oppose Him. They had already failed again and again, in their attempts to silence Him. But they could not let Him work unhindered. It was preposterous that an unauthorised teacher from Galilee should triumph over them, the recognised and revered leaders of the nation. Something must be found against Him. As the enemies of Daniel felt that they would find nothing against him

except "as concerning the law of his God," so the Scribes and Pharisees seem to have thought that they would find nothing against Jesus except as concerning His characteristic tenderness to those whom they called sinners. That feature of His life was peculiar to Him. It had surprised and even shocked them. Here, if anywhere, was His weakness. It is a remarkable testimony to the truth of the general trend of the life and teaching of Jesus that His foes planned an attack like this against Him. They are convincing, but unwilling, witnesses to the genuineness of the Gospel history.

There was no lack of skill in the method of assault. If, as they expected, He said that the woman should not be stoned, they would be able to accuse Him as a despiser of the Law of Moses, as a foe to the sacredness of marriage, as an encourager of loose living. They would have supported their accusation by recalling His familiarities with publicans and sinners, and might have been able to convince the multitude of its truth. In the East, nothing so easily arouses suspicion or awakens hostility as a matter that touches, or seems to touch, the honour of the family. Let one word be spoken by Jesus that could, by any ingenuity, be turned or twisted into an admission that the Law of Moses was too severe in its treatment of the sin of adultery, and at once His popularity would perish. The manhood of the nation would range itself against Him. The respect and admiration in which He was held would be changed to condemnation and bitter opposition.

The Scribes and Pharisees did not think that He could avoid playing into their hands. He had so constantly manifested a spirit of charity in dealing with sinners that it seemed impossible, in replying to the question which they had submitted, that He could deny Himself and say what was inconsistent with the pervading spirit of His teaching. They were counting on the consistency of Jesus. He must either speak as He had never spoken, or deliver Himself into their hands as One who regarded with lightness the sin that dishonoured and destroyed the life of the home. It was a subtle and cleverly contrived dilemma.

2. Jesus met the question in a most unusual way. He "stooped down and with His finger wrote on the ground." We do not think that He did so that He might gain time to consider His answer. He who never faltered elsewhere would not falter here. Professor Seeley* suggests that it was a feeling of intolerable shame that led Him to hide His face. To a pure spirit there is no pain equal to that which comes from close contact with evil. It is not easy for us even to read aloud the story of this incident—what must have been the

* "Ecce Homo."

The First Stone

feelings of Jesus as the shameful fact was forced upon Him—and forced upon Him in such a way ? Surely these men, professors of righteousness though they were, had no glimmer of the shame of their conduct. They had no feeling of delicacy in speaking of the sin of the woman. She had been "taken in adultery, *in the very act.*" They added that touch of scarlet to her crimson sin. They mouthed the phrase as if it were a sweet morsel. There could be escape for Jesus by appealing for proof. Openly, bluntly, almost triumphantly, they told out the deed of sin and shame. They had no thought of the woman suffering the agonies of exposure in the unshaded courts of the Temple. She had ceased to be a woman to them. She was only "such" an one—a criminal—a case. They said nothing of the man, the *fellowman* who had been the partner of her guilt. He had escaped, as he so often does.

It was only of the woman whom they dragged into the scorching publicity of the Temple, whose dishonour they proclaimed with unbated breath. " I hold it sin," said Caleb Garth, " to expose a man's sin unless I'm clear that it must be done to save the innocent."* But these men did all this that they might entrap the innocent. The woman's sin was of little account to them except as a means of

* " Middlemarch."

catching Jesus. The shameless callousness of their deed was enough to make the Saviour hide His face. The accusers were worse than the accused. Her sin was born of passion ; theirs of malignant cunning. Jesus could not look upon it. He hid His face from the men, not from the woman. His silence and posture were a rebuke to them.

But the Scribes and Pharisees did not take them so. His action seems to have suggested the triumphant thought that He was caught at last. Eager to win the fruits of their victory, they pressed their question upon Him again and again. But He only lifted up His head and said, " He that is without sin among you, let him first cast a stone at her," and then stooped again to write. That was His answer. " The bird had escaped out of the snare of the fowler." How wisely, how pregnantly, how piercingly did He reply ! He did not question the Law or their statement of it. He said nothing about its severity, nor proposed to modify it in any way. Not a word fell from His lips which could be construed into an attack on the sanctity of the home. He also said nothing that was inconsistent with His characteristic tenderness towards sinners. Few as His words were, they were sufficient to turn their thoughts from Himself and the woman to themselves. He carried the war right into the heart of the camp of the enemy. He said,

The First Stone

" He that is without sin among you, let him first cast a stone at her."

3. In this reply we notice that our Lord maintained His usual attitude of independence regarding the administration of the Law. On another occasion, when a similar question of legal right was submitted to Him, He refused to interfere. He said, " Who made me a judge or a divider over you ? " He took up the same position in this case. He would not enter into the discussion of questions that belonged to a judge.

He lifted the matter out of the legal relation in which the Scribes and Pharisees had looked at it, and set it in relation to a higher law of personal life which they had forgotten. The judge before whom such a case was brought must guide himself by the law which he had been appointed to administer. But the Scribes and Pharisees were not judges. They were private citizens, meeting not in a court of justice, but in a public place. That fact brought them into a different relation to the woman whom they were accusing. It was not the Law of Moses which was to guide them, but the law of personal life. Judgment by the law of the land must still go on. It was not abrogated, or modified. The magistrate, the master, the parent must still perform their duties, and fulfil the responsibilities of the relation which they held to those who were under their charge. But when private persons deal with those who have sinned, they must act in accordance with this great principle which exercises its authority in the hearts of men,—" He that is without sin among you, let him first cast a stone at her." The Saviour's words are in harmony with all His teaching elsewhere respecting private judgment. We are to judge ourselves first, and the judgment must at least be as severe as that by which others are tried. The accusers of the woman were forgetting this. They were treating her as if they were not sinners. Their own spiritual condition should have been a matter of first importance to them, but it gave them no concern. Their callousness and malignancy, the sins which they had done and forgotten, rendered them unfit for the office they had assumed. Jesus gave them a new perspective. He bade them think of themselves : He turned their thoughts to their own sins. His teaching here is in line with the precepts of the Apostle which was derived from Him : " Brethren, if any man be overtaken in a fault, ye which are spiritual, restore such an one in the spirit of meekness, considering thyself, lest thou also be tempted " (Gal. vi. 1). Contempt and hardness are the last things which sinners should show to sinners. It is not enough to say that the judgment is deserved. Our fitness to pronounce it has also to be considered.

The First Stone

Our Lord does not say, " He that is free from the sin of the woman, let him first cast a stone at her." We cannot believe that the Scribes and Pharisees were all secret adulterers. But exemption from a particular form of sin does not give the right to judge those who have been guilty of it. It is a constant tendency of men to be harsh regarding sins they themselves have not done. People in positions of respectability, such as the Scribes and Pharisees, are prone to speak strongly of the sins of the outcast and the ignorant. Their own lives are generally free from the open vices into which the outcasts have fallen. But the worst sins are not those which are vicious and glaring. The sins of the mind are as heinous as the sins of the flesh, and sometimes more so. It is easy to thank God that we are not as other men, whose sins are open and known. The vicious and the drunken may be harshly condemned by those who in God's sight are more deserving of condemnation. It is as sinners that we are to judge sinners : and if we remember that we shall cease to judge them. We shall only be just and merciful when we remember these great principles— that we are to think of our own sins first, and that our judgment, if it is exercised, is not for condemnation, but restoration.

4. But there is more here than the judgment of sin. To cast the first stone was to begin the

punishment of sin. Judgment is indeed part of sin's penalty, and it is hard to bear. Sometimes even criticism is more than we can stand. But punishment is usually regarded as something that follows judgment. Our Lord does not forbid the Scribes and Pharisees inflicting the sentence which the Law of Moses ordained for the sin in question. He only says that they are to see to it that they are fit for the awful act, and by doing so He made it impossible. He is still holding them to the position of private persons. The magistrate may inflict such a penalty on the criminal, but one thing only to the Saviour's mind can give a private individual the right to punish sin. He must have something of the holiness of God. " He that is without sin among you, let him cast the first stone at her." Thus we are taught that the punishment of *sin* is only safe in sinless hands. The crime, the breach of social or family order, remains in the hands of the magistrate or the parent, but sinners have no place in the punishment of sinners. This is part of the gracious mercy of the Gospel. Sinners may plead for sinners ; but God alone can punish them.

5. Again He stooped and wrote upon the ground. What did He write ? The question has often been asked, for this is the only occasion on which it is said that He wrote anything. If this incident had

not been recorded, we should not even have known that He could write. One manuscript* has the suggestive variation, that when He stooped the second time He wrote on the ground "the sins of each of them." It may have been so. The Scribes and Pharisees may have thought that they were without sin, even as St. Paul once, as a Pharisee, boasted that " as touching the righteousness of the Law " he was " blameless." Possibly nothing but a direct statement of personal guilt or secret sin could penetrate their confidence or disturb their complacency. So one interpreter† imagines that Jesus wrote, " Eldad stole the house of Joram's widow." When Eldad read the words, he turned and went away. Nahum came next, and the finger traced the accusing words, " Nahum slew Azidad in the desert," and he, too, turned and went away. And so with each one unto the youngest. It may have been so, but we think not. We rather believe that it was the words of Jesus, spoken as He alone could speak, and the look by which they were accompanied, that overcame them. " Never man spake like this Man." Never man " looked " like this Man. He was a " discerner of the thoughts and intents of the heart." The power of the " seer " was His in its completest perfection, and His words

* See Nestle's " Greek Testament " *in loco.*

† Prof. Caspar René Gregory, *Biblical World*, November, 1898.

were like a " sharp two-edged sword." Nothing is more remarkable in the story of His ministry than the unerring accuracy with which He touched the secrets of the lives of men. " Go call thy husband," " Sell what thou hast," were as the touch of Ithuriel's spear to the Woman of Samaria and the rich young Ruler. With the words, " He that is without sin among you, let him cast the first stone," He struck at the conscience of these Scribes and Pharisees, and His blow went home. These men were sinners, and they never had realised it before. Their own hearts condemned them now, and they went away from the accusing silence. They thought no more of the woman's sin, or of their plan of " catching " Jesus. It was He who had caught them. Jesus is still the Lord of the conscience. It is His abiding witness in the hearts of men. When we come into His presence, we feel that " He knows our works," and that He makes us know them, too. However men may disregard the sting of conscience ; however they may seek to silence its voice, or sear its delicate sensibilities, it always answers to His appeal. Sometimes it is the silence of Jesus which overwhelms us as we pray. It is more terrible than His words.

But the grace which gives a conviction of sin may be received in vain. The Scribes and Pharisees went away convicted but not repentant. They maintained their opposition to Jesus in a more concentrated and hostile form. Their defeat increased their hatred, till it could be satisfied with nothing but His death.

6. The accusers went away; Jesus was left alone with the woman. He asked, " Where are thine accusers ? Hath no man condemned thee ? " She answered, " No man." Then came to her the great surprise—" Neither do I condemn thee ; go, and sin no more." As this woman saw how her accusers, men of rigid morality and stainless reputation, had gone away unable to bear the words and the silence of Jesus, she must surely have wondered what He would say to her. Did it amaze her that He did not condemn, or even upbraid, her ? Did she understand the mercy and the severity of the words He addressed to her, or did she leave that awful presence glad that she had escaped so easily ? We cannot tell. There is always the dreadful possibility that the grace of God may be received in vain. Jesus had refused to be her judge. The sinful had condemned her without pity ; the sinless One spoke words of mercy. The time of judgment was not yet. He had not come to judge but to save, and He pointed out the way of salvation to her. It was the day of grace and opportunity.

Surely it was with a repentent and resolute spirit that she went away ! Hard as the nether millstone must her heart have been if it was not broken into penitence and gratitude by the tenderness and hopefulness of Jesus. Must not His purity have filled her with loathing of herself and her sin ? He had delivered her from the cruel hands of her accusers, but that was not all. He had said, " Sin no more." Surely that meant that there was hope for her ; that a new life was possible ; that He believed it or He would never have said it. Whether she saw it or not we know that that is the faith of Jesus. He ever saw " the best glimmer in the worst." Hope burned in Him when it had died out of other men. The lost could be saved ; the sinner could " sin no more."

That is the faith we must ever cherish for ourselves, and seek to kindle in the hearts of the sinful and despairing. " He is able to save unto the uttermost all who come unto God by Him." Since He had hope for this sinful woman, who is there for whom hope must be abandoned ?